Someone Else's CHILD

DEBBIE BELL

Ordering Information:

Prime Seven Media
518 Landmann St.
Tomah City, WI 54660

Printed in the United States of America

Dedicated to Derlerean

For you to understand the long journey
You need to know where I have been

Your loving Mummy

A big thank you to family and friends for their
encouragement and support.

A very special thank you to Moira, for her time and dedication
during the writing of this story and Print DNA for its production.

FOREWORD

If you were in a supermarket and passed Debbie and Derlerean, you understandably would just think they were an average mother and son out doing a bit of shopping. After reading their story, I'm sure "average" is the last word you would think of to describe them. This is a must read account of one persons sheer determination to succeed regardless of what obstacles are put in the way.

You will laugh, cry, get angry, be embarrassed, excited, relieved, but mostly be inspired by the contents of these pages.

Thank you Debbie, I have grown as a person through reading your story.

Ian Andrews

I have felt for some time that I would try to write a small book about my life for two reasons, the first being that regardless of what you have been through when you are young you can still make a go of it when you reach adulthood, and secondly a lot of people don't realise just how lucky they have been and how much they have to be grateful for.

I was born in April 1961 to parents who I believe married for the wrong reasons and they were not mature enough to have a solid relationship. My father Barry had come from a home where his father had gone to the War as a soldier and, like plenty of others, came back a different man as a result of what he had been through. His mother seemed to be a very nice lady and also his sister seemed like her mother; someone that you wouldn't mind getting to know. For some reason, which I will never understand, my father never got on with his dad at all. There seemed to be a total lack of communication between them and this created a lot of problems. What had never been mentioned to me by my paternal grandparents is that my father was made a Ward of the State of Victoria from 11th November 1951 until 10th June 1954. During that time, he was given a different name. The reason given was that he was neglected. It's a little difficult for me to picture his mum neglecting him, but on the other hand, I don't have a problem seeing his dad neglecting him, because of his attitude. What I saw in my grandfather during the last years that I was visiting him, was that he had no time for his son to the point that one day I said to him "how on earth will you get on with him if you are not prepared to listen"? After I asked this question of my grandfather, I thought to myself, am I nuts or something? Here was I sticking up for a man I would possibly never meet, but that's the way I am.

Even though I have been through a lot that is one of the things that I can't stand; that people are not given the opportunity to be heard and at least give their view on any issue. As for my mother Barbara, she comes from a different background, one from which she wanted to escape due to the way things were at home. She was the youngest of three children and they grew up mainly in the country.

My parents married in November 1959 in Adelaide, South Australia, against the wishes of my mother's parents, even though both parents signed the Marriage Certificate. My Aunty who was to later look after me for a while, held a small reception at her home and then the newlyweds went to live at Tailem Bend in South Australia for a short time before they moved on due to my dad's wandering ways. During that time, Barry had jobs truck driving as well as working for the South Australia Railways Department until he was dismissed. While in Tailem Bend my oldest brother Peter was born in July, the brother who I would not meet until I was at least fifteen years of age.

In April of the next year, I was born in Adelaide at the Queen Elizabeth Hospital. I was born with an extra thumb on my right hand which was to remain until I was six years of age. I am not very clear about what happened over the next year, but I know my aunty who was living in Adelaide raising her own family, looked after me for some time, helping out my mother. From what I understand, sometime in 1961 our family moved down to Mount Gambier. I'm not sure why but I guess it was for work reasons. While we were there, two female Police Officers checked out the place that we were in because they had been tipped off that things were not as they should have been. This included taking photos of me because I was not being looked after and as a result, I was underweight. The charges were dropped and things seemed to improve. Later that year my parents moved from Mount Gambier, leaving me behind in the hospital.

It seems that things had not really improved at all. On the 2nd August 1962, The Community Welfare Department (as it was known at the time) received an official complaint regarding the way I was being treated. It was noted however, that my brothers Peter and new brother Darryl (who had just been born the month before), seemed to have been treated quite reasonably.

I was to come under the care of the Welfare on the 18th February, 1963 and I was taken to a Children's Home later in March. Barry deserted his responsibility to his young family again on the 8th of July that year, leaving my mother with my older brother Peter and my younger brother Darryl.

On the 9th December that same year, Barbara went to live with my Aunty and her husband and that's where she had an interview with Mr Thomas Wood. My mother was asked if she was a deserted wife and the answer to that question was yes. How long? Five months. Have you heard from your husband? No. Barbara then went on to explain that she couldn't have me at her sister's place because she already had two boys and she was only getting an allowance of six pound a week or a fortnight. By March 1963 my father had clocked up six convictions for not paying his bills. In the February, my mother notified the Community Welfare Department that she had to have an operation on her arm on the 27th, and she was in no condition to look after me as a result. On the 17th February, 1964, I was officially put up for adoption by my mother without my father's knowledge. The adoption order didn't do much good as Barry refused to sign it when he found out. He was in jail at the time and his Probation Officer asked him if he was aware of the fact that he had a child up for adoption, and his answer was NO! Regardless of my parent's faults, I will always believe that it should have been a joint decision.

I was placed in the care of the Morris family who were at that stage living at Jubuk which is a small country community in the area of the Mallee near Murray Bridge. The Welfare had been given this address on the 14th April, 1964, not very long before my third birthday. When I went to join the Morris family, I gained a foster brother named Johnathon who was just a year older than me. It didn't take too long to know that he was being favoured and as a result he was being treated a lot better than me. I can remember a lot of times when we would be doing the same things and he would get better care and more attention than me. Most times I would be bathed in the kitchen sink and Johnathon would always have his bath in the bathroom, maybe because I was small enough to fit. I was still very much underweight for my age. Afterwards they would dry me on the table and for some reason this sticks in my mind. I think they may have been smoking.

It seems that behind the scenes, there were people looking at adopting me, namely Mr and Mrs Jackson, but on the 24th April, 1964 they notified the Department that they were no longer interested, so that was the end of that effort to find me a permanent home. For some reason in my file, it was noted on the 21st February, that I had two thumbs on my right hand. Hey—how slow were they to notice? I had known all the time because I used it to hold my pencils and eating utensils without using any other fingers. Also, it was noted that it was not known if I had any of my immunisations at this stage, so who knows what was or what wasn't done.

Just before my birthday in April, it was decided that I would need to take milk emulsion (yummy) for some time to try and build up my strength and immune system. It seems I managed to catch every cold and I had frequent bouts of pneumonia for which I would end up in the Children's Hospital. In June 1964, I must have had a real bad cold and cough as I was taken to see Dr. Crafter and I remember he had grey hair so he must have been old in the eyes of a six year old. By August there was very little improvement so I had to continue the tablets that I had been given.

At last the Welfare was starting to take some notice of what was happening in the Morris household. On the 13th March, 1965 I was attended by a doctor at the Sturt Clinic because of a fall. My chin had become very bruised and swollen so x-rays were done at the Adelaide

Children's Hospital. For some reason this must have been very traumatic as I honestly cannot remember it happening, even though I was nearly four years old. It was noted in my file that the Welfare Department were not so sure that this had been an accident as Mrs Morris had advised them, so goodness knows what really happened that day. On Friday 27th August, I was taken to see a Dr. Edhouse at the Children's Hospital because I was creating serious problems for my present foster mother although I have no idea what they were. I wasn't in the best position that a child could be in.

By this time I was going to Sunday school at the Christian Revival Centre on Sturt Road, which I didn't mind as I enjoyed colouring in the drawing afterwards at home using my extra thumb. I don't remember what the occasion was, but one Sunday, we had to sing for the adults up on the stage. I didn't enjoy it as I had to sit beside this stupid boy who seemed to get a lot of pleasure out of bugging me by pulling down my brand new knee high white socks. I was always really happy when I got something new and besides, I knew that if the elastic got stretched when the socks were still quite new that I would be in trouble when I got home. To me, Mrs Morris was very fussy about little things that really were not very important when you boiled it all down. I can remember once she had bought me a red plastic imitation carpet sweeper and she said that it was not allowed to touch the footpath. We walked to the shopping centre which seemed to be a real long way. I can remember this very well as my new toy felt so heavy; maybe it was because I was not very strong due to my poor physical condition. Then another time I managed to lose one of the buttons off my coat at kindergarten and did I cop it that time.

About Seven Years Old

Regardless of this, it seems that my foster mother was getting attached to me as she mentioned to the Welfare that I was a dear little girl even though I didn't have a lot to say, but it seems that I would give her some smiles. Things were not always bad where I was living, I can remember being taken to the beach on hot days and that's where I acquired a very strong dislike for beach umbrellas. Once we were using ours and as luck would have it a gust of wind came up and blew the stupid thing on top of my ankle and to this day, I have a scar to remind me of that particular outing. I don't remember what beach it was but we would be taken for drives along the sand in what I remember was our big black family car. Maybe it seemed to be so big because Johnathan and I were only very young at the time. Another outing we went on must have been to Port Adelaide. We went on what seemed to be a huge ship and we were given a tour of the inside and shown how the cargo deck worked. On real hot days Johnathon and I would jump off the veranda rail into the sprinkler to keep cool, which was a lot of fun.

On 26th November, 1965 the Morris's notified the Department that they had changed their minds about returning me to the Welfare, so things must have been improving. At this time we were living in Kingswood, a suburb of Adelaide, only a couple of houses from my foster dad's mother's place—Mrs Ryan. I can just see her now, sitting in her old chair looking at me and asking me how I was. She was a real nice old lady, and even though I knew that she wasn't my real grandma, she was good enough for me and I could just run along to her place when I was allowed to.

One day when I was visiting her she looked at me and asked "have you fallen over today Debbie?" I do remember on this occasion that I replied "No". I still can still picture her face and for some reason it made me feel sad. She may have had some idea of what was going on at home. I feel that she knew something because I constantly had bruises on me. It seems that Grandma Ryan was not the only one taking notice of what was going on. Mrs Reed who lived over the road had lodged a complaint with the Welfare, saying that I was often smacked for no apparent reason. I can't remember Mr Morris doing the hitting as I think he was out most of the time.

Just before Christmas 1966 I was sitting on the bedroom floor putting on my socks, as I had been told to by my foster mum, while she was making the beds. She must have been having a bad day because instead of telling me to move, she just moved the bed and managed to hit me in the side of the head and split open my left ear. Her husband (who never saw it happen), had to rush me to the doctor on the front of his pushbike to have some stitches put in. It bled so much that they had to suck the blood out of my ear canal. To this day I don't believe that Mrs Morris ever felt bad about it and she will never know how lucky she was that the Welfare didn't pick up that it wasn't just an accident which is what she told me. I have known all along that it never was.

Sometimes Mr Morris would come into my bedroom at night when the light was out and hold me down on the bed. I used to rock myself to try and get away from him, but it was pretty useless and I couldn't do anything about it.

For one Christmas I did get a really nice blue wooden dolls bed that I was really proud of and I would always copy the others when the beds were getting made. I managed to keep it until I reached adulthood. I hoped that one day I might have a little girl of my own who could enjoy using it as much as I did. Johnathan and I must have kept our parents very busy. We both managed to get the measles in the early part of the New Year. Hey, at least we were the same this time, nothing like adding to the list of sicknesses. I had only just had the mumps the November before.

My spare thumb was finally removed early in May 1967 at the Adelaide Children's Hospital, while I was under the Welfare's supervision at Seaforth Home. Afterwards, I was to return to my foster parents. Mrs Morris had the awful job of keeping the bandages on me, but they kept slipping off. This was most likely caused by the bent shape of my remaining thumb. I did learn a couple of things during this period; for one thing, I discovered that I had a terrible dislike for anything that resembled a vacuum cleaner. My foster mum would chase me in the house with hers and I was scared that I would be sucked up. It might seem stupid to an adult, but it can be very real to a small child. Every time I saw the lady with the floor polisher come anywhere near my room in the hospital I managed to spring up onto my bed with only one hand, a feat I could not normally have achieved. Secondly, doesn't it drive you crazy when you have a heap of stitches that are very itchy because the wound is healing, and you MUST not scratch them or else? I was really pleased when finally all the stitches had been removed. The stitches left what look like an oversized zigzag pattern, but it doesn't bother me. I had expected that my remaining thumb would be a lot straighter than it was before but never mind, at least I could now learn to use my other fingers like everybody else.

I never minded going to the hospital as I would get looked after by some really nice nurses. Sometimes even before I was taken to the room where I would be staying, I was minded by the staff behind the big counter until one of the nurses would come to pick me up.

The people from the welfare didn't make a habit of hanging around to make sure I was really settled in. All of this time I can just remember seeing Johnathan looking very pale. Goodness only knows what was wrong with him. Maybe we were both in the same boat and we should have never been there to start with, but kids don't seem to have any say when it comes to situations like this. I just hope that by now the Department continues to learn from the lessons of the past 30 years.

Quite frequently Uncle Ted (as I would call him) would come to take my foster dad out for what seemed to be all of Sunday afternoon. I can remember it so well because he would always bring with him a bottle of Coke and some chips for us two kids. Other than this, I don't have too many memories of him, and I don't remember him coming over with a lady, so maybe he wasn't married or his wife stayed at home all the time.

Sometime during the next few months, I must have been back at Seaforth House for a while as it's mentioned in my file that Mrs Morris seemed to be feeling guilty about me returning to them. On 17th August, 1967 the welfare department finally realised that the situation was out of control.

Apparently Mrs Morris suffered from nerve problems and it seems that she was taking it out on me. I have no memory of what led up to this, but I know one thing and that is that I was taken away in an awful hurry with no suitcase or anything else that was mine, except for my bear. On 21st August I was taken back to Seaforth Home and from then on the Morris's were declared unsuitable for any more foster care. I have no idea of whatever happened to Johnathan, I just hope that he made it through everything until he could choose for himself.

It seems that regardless of all the commotion and anything else that happened that day, I thought that I was going on a holiday. I can still remember going down the street in what seemed to me a real big car. I was taken to get some new clothes because I was going to stay with my kindergarten teacher, Miss Lilywhite, for a few days. She must have been a very kind lady to offer to look after me. She told the welfare that she didn't want me to feel rejected. By the end of September, Mrs Morris finally admitted that she would lose her temper and hit me. I can't remember those occasions, or why she would do it, but I know for one thing that still to this day I can't stand seeing children hit anywhere else except on their bum, and for some unknown reason, I don't like being around people who are drinking alcohol. I'm not sure if it's the smell or what, but maybe something bad happened to me while I was in that type of environment. In September, 1967 it was time for me to go and have my hernia fixed up, so off I went with my best friend, Bear.

I don't remember a lot about this stay in the hospital, but I can still see in my mind, the face of a really nice nurse with big brown eyes who had to give me an injection and she was kind enough to say sorry. Maybe this stuck in my mind as it was not a word I had heard very often.

After I left hospital I was taken back to the Children's home where I was given special attention for once, as a result of my operation. I couldn't sit in the bath because I still had a bandage on the wound and it had to remain there until all the stitches were ready to be removed and then things were back to normal.

By this stage, I was starting to stick up for myself around the other kids who I was living with. We seemed to have a big play area which included a large lawn, bikes and other play equipment which sometimes we would fight over, and if we got caught, we had to have a time out. Sometimes we would even go over to the big kids play area which normally was off limits. There was one very important rule regarding the use of the bikes and that was there was to be no riding them on the lawn. I soon learnt to grab every opportunity to run and tell when someone had broken the rules so I would have a turn. How nasty can a sweet little six year old girl get? I can still see the horrified look on the lady's face when she caught all of us girls jumping on our beds. I can remember that we had decided to do it, just to see how long before we would be caught. It didn't matter; we still had plenty of enjoyment out of it. Sometimes I would just lie on my bed looking up at the ceiling, just to check out where the spiders were going because they would move around the room during the night and then we would have to find out where they had made their new home in the morning. I'll be honest, I really didn't like them being over my bed as I was scared that they would fall on me during the night.

On the 8th November, 1967, I was taken to say goodbye to the other children again, but this time I knew it was different because I had been dressed up in a new sailor dress which was special in itself as I wouldn't normally get to wear new clothes. Every time a child was leaving and not coming back, they would come to say goodbye when we were having a story read to us. Well, now it was my turn. I didn't know where I was going, but I was just happy to go with my social worker, Miss Sewall, in her car. We ended up at the Adelaide Airport which was a big outing, as I had never been there before. It was a bit overwhelming to see all the people, let alone the planes as well. I was introduced to a lady who was to be my new foster mother and I was told that I would be going on the plane with her to Kangaroo Island which is off the South Australian coast, just below Adelaide. This would turn out to be my home for the next 20 years.

The house in Kingscote, Kangaroo Island

Well, my new foster mum must have had a heart of gold as she had never seen me in her life before and she had never even been told anything about me before she agreed to become my new mum. What had happened before this was that another couple were meant to have me, but the welfare managed to get their surnames confused and by the time it was sorted out, it was too late as they had already been given two other children and they felt that they couldn't manage with any more. The wife of the couple knew my new mum personally and had asked her if she was at all interested in getting a foster child. After what must have been quite a bit of thinking and I dare say, saying her prayers, (mum is very spiritual), she agreed that a social worker could come and visit her while she was in Adelaide. About three months after returning to Kangaroo Island she received a phone call to tell her that I was now ready to be picked up. So it was arranged that I would be collected early in November when she had to come over to Adelaide for an appointment. I don't remember too much about the trip on the plane as I slept most of the way.

To get to Kingscote, the biggest town on Kangaroo Island where my new home was to be, we had to drive a fair way until we ended up at what seemed to me to be a huge stone house. While my new mum was getting tea ready, I laid down in her room for a while. I don't really remember what she gave me to eat, but I do know that I told her very clearly that it was not nice! I dare say she would have been wondering what she had brought home with her. After tea I went out with her to what would become weekly bible study, at which time I had another sleep after looking at all the strange faces. Over the next few days, as well as trying to get to know my new mum, I found my way around the house and yard. By day three I must have had the feeling that I was staying there as I said to her, "if you call me darling, I'll call you Mummy".

As the next few months passed, Mum had to teach me how to hop, skip and a few other things that I should have been able to do at my age. Also my speech needed a lot of correction as I couldn't say my 'f's or 's's, so as you can imagine, things that we say mostly every day, would have sounded quite funny to anyone who was listening. The next year I started school which was at the end of our street so it wasn't very far for me to walk. I had some problems with my schooling because the doctors in Adelaide had put me on sedatives. Mum soon took me off them as they were doing more harm than good and it's beyond me how stupid somebody could be, to put a six year old child on this sort of medication when the child's problems are being caused by circumstances beyond their control.

It did not take me very long to get myself a permanent group of friends who I would spend time with during recess. Most of these kids would continue to be in the same class as me until I left when I was sixteen.

After about eighteen months living with my new foster mum, she became very sick with what is known as Bell's palsy, which affects the muscles in the face. I had to spend quite a while with my new aunties while mum was in the hospital. I used to be taken to see mum while she was in the hospital on Sunday afternoons and I would wear a patch on the same eye as mum, and sit on her bed with her. During this period of time I was being looked after by Mum's youngest brother and his wife who had three children of their own, and as far as I remember, I didn't mind being there.

In June of that year my newly acquired sister got married in Mount Barker and Mum was just well enough to make it to the wedding. We went with Mum's youngest sister and her husband. It seemed a long way to me and my outfit was a light blue twin set and a white pleated skirt. Mum and I went to the home where the bride was getting ready as she wanted me to be in some of the photos. It seems quite funny now because Mum had bought these silly white gloves for me to wear, and she was having trouble getting them on me. At last the photographer had had enough, so they didn't get put on at all. During the wedding ceremony I felt very sad for some reason; I had a feeling that I would never see the bride again. After mum got out of the hospital I went to the Seaton Primary School. I can remember the Education Department sent someone around to see why I was not attending school. They must have been satisfied with the answers as I can't remember them coming back. At home things did not take too long to get back to the normal routine. Mum used to take me fishing with her sister and husband who lived not far out of Kingscote and sometimes we would go by ourselves. One thing that I really hated was when it would be getting really cold and rainy and mum would say I just want to catch a few more! I guess it's always more interesting when you're the one who is catching the fish.

About Eight Years Old

When I was nine, it was discovered just how bad my vision was and so I was taken to get fitted with contact lenses. Who knows why they didn't give me glasses just like everybody else, it was a big thing for me to have to put in the stupid things every day. It was made worse by the fact that my eyes would get irritated very easily to the point that I would not be able to open them because of the wind or brightness of the sun. As a present for saying that I would try to do my best in wearing them, mum gave me a new bike which I really liked. The first time I rode it on the road was down the hill (big mistake) to show mum's friends, who had known her for many years. Well, guess what? I forgot to use the brakes and instead of putting them on with the pedals, I put my foot down on the ground to stop and I ended up falling and spinning on my hip. I wasn't too happy as I had to be taken to the hospital to have the wound and scratches fixed up. The wound left a scar so wide that it's a constant reminder of the occasion, and definite proof that skin and road surfaces don't mix.

Well, the years went by and nothing out of the ordinary happened that is really worth mentioning.

In February 1976, the community welfare received a letter from the equivalent department in Queensland regarding my two brothers, who until now I didn't know existed. Mum had never been told any of my background when she first fostered me, so it was a surprise to both of us. One day she said to me "what would you do if you had two brothers?"

Seeing as I thought it was a general question, I didn't give much thought to my reply and just said "are they like me?" Poor thing, she had been given the task of trying to get some sort of reaction and then having to tell me about them. Maybe it was my happy go lucky nature that got me through this first stage. I didn't give much thought to what she said, as after all—I had been an only child for a long time, and so to me it would not make too much difference. I was used to being alone because Mum's two grown up kids had left home just before I had arrived on the scene. It was some time before I noticed there was an unopened letter which was addressed to me on the fridge, but for some unknown reason, I was not in any rush to open it which normally I would be when I received mail. One day mum said to me "aren't you going to open your letter Debbie?" and she went on to explain that it was from my two brothers. The boys had written an introductory letter to me, telling me about themselves and what they liked to do for hobbies etc. For some reason I wasn't too surprised, as I had sometimes wondered if I had any relations.

Mum decided that she would take me to Dalby in Queensland to visit them in the winter, but this didn't get me out of doing school work. The teacher was kind enough to send some along with me so I wouldn't get behind too much.

Peter and Darryl were living in a big Boys Home which was run like a normal home with house parents who were a married couple. After we had settled in to where we were staying, just out of Dalby, the lady of the house took us to the Boys Home. When we got to the door, a lot of thoughts were running through my mind. I had no idea of what my two brothers would look like, or their personalities. When mum and I were taken into the lounge room all of the boys were sitting on the floor. I guess that was the easiest way of doing it. There were many different faces looking at us, but only two of them knew who I was. I think it was the lady who told Peter and Darryl to stand up. It was only then that I knew which ones were my two brothers. The others were dismissed from the room while we were introduced to each other. After a while, mum was taken into the office. Apparently my father had written a letter asking to see me, if I would agree. An experience like this is very hard to explain on paper, as you have no idea what is running through somebody else's mind and how they will react. Besides feeling very timid, I spent most of the time wondering what was going to happen next as I knew that my life would now include my two brothers if it all worked out the right way.

My first meeting with Darryl and Peter at Dalby about 1976

While we were there, it was decided that Peter and Darryl would come out to stay with us for a week, seeing as it was their school holidays. This would give us a bit of time to get to know each other. It didn't take too much time to work out that Darryl and I clashed very easily, but on the other hand Peter and I got on very well. On the night that we had been to see the boys for the first time poor mum had to ask me if I was interested in seeing my father. That was just too much because I had only just seen my brothers for the first time, and there comes a time when enough is enough, so my answer was NO! I had a bad night and I cried my eyes out and to my dismay I simply didn't wake up twice to go to the toilet which only made me feel worse. I couldn't cope with the thought of meeting another stranger who was meant to be my Father. Our week together was not too bad until we got the flu. The people in the home had it first and then we got it. We had been asked out to a friend's place so we could meet their family and we soon found out that it's difficult to fit in visits with the flu.

A couple of days after the boys returned to school and we left Dalby to come home via Melbourne because we were going to visit mum's brother. It wasn't easy to say goodbye because I didn't know what would be in the future for us. Darryl wanted to swap places with me, but that wasn't on, as Mum was a widow and he was better off staying where he was with Peter.

I only had a few more years to go in school, but I wasn't really sure of what I would like to do when I left. Any dreams of getting a proper job were shattered one day when one of Mum's so called friends came to visit. I really can't remember the conversation too well, but he told mum that girls don't need higher education. Great, I thought, as I saw the end of my school days flash before my eyes. For some stupid reason, mum believed everything that this person said. It can create a problem when you only have one parent and as much as I tried to tell her that I wanted to finish school, the answer was NO! From that day I lost interest in my school work to the point that it got so bad the teacher told mum I wouldn't be able to finish high school anyway. The teacher had no idea of what was going on at home, so no wonder he had such a bad opinion of my school work. Out of frustration, I went through all of my best school work which I had been keeping, and burned it which later I would regret. I couldn't cope with it being in the house because it reminded me of what I couldn't continue to do. I felt sad as I really did enjoy going to school, but there wasn't a thing I could do about it. I knew that if I approached my social worker, I would have been in very serious trouble, because by now mum had started saying that if I wasn't happy there that I should go somewhere else and of course, I had nowhere else to go.

I started to apply for a few jobs that came up, but no luck. It's not that easy to get a job when you're living on an island, especially if you're not related to anyone that owns a business.

The year after I left school it was discovered that I needed to have some surgery on my face, to repair the bone structure which had not fully developed. Mum had taken me to the doctor when she had noticed that my lips would turn blue while I was sleeping. She knew there must be a problem but she didn't know just how bad it was until we were sent to the ear, nose and throat specialist. The poor doctor took one look at my face and realised that I could have a bigger problem then we originally thought. I was then referred to see the head doctor of the Australian Facial Cranial Unit for an assessment. After I had been through numerous tests and x-rays, it was time to go to see what was going to be done for me. It was quite a nerve wracking experience for both of us, because it didn't feel too good when I had this room full of people looking at me who knew more about me than I did about them. The first doctor that I had seen was away on holidays, so there was not a lot to be said. Needless to say I did get upset as I had no idea what they wanted to do to me or how it was to be done.

The silence in the room was very hard to handle as I felt like a piece of artwork being judged by everybody. And hey, it's not every day that you get somebody that you don't know very well, running his finger up and down your spine! I guess it was his way of trying to make the whole experience not so traumatic; after all I was only seventeen.

Finally, I had the operation done in a really nice private hospital. The pain wasn't too bad. I didn't have any feeling in my face at all as the nerves had been cut, but my rib cage was another story. It always hurts more where the bone is taken from than where it's put. Not many people can say that they have got a piece of rib in their nose, but never mind, nothing like being different! They had to use some of the rib bone to build up the nose so the air flow would be increased and also just above my top jaw line. They said if this wasn't done that my face would fall in faster than normal when I reached old age.

It was quite funny being in the hospital as you see all sorts of people. There was only one lady who was quite a bit older than me and I soon got the impression that she thought quite a bit of herself because she had had some plastic surgery done on her nose. As far as I could see, there was nothing wrong with it to start with and I soon noticed that every time I went for my walks up and down the passageway for some exercise, there she was, standing in front of the mirror. It struck me as quite funny and one of the nurses had made a comment to me that they should have just put a paper bag over her head with a couple of holes in it so she could see where she was going!

After we had been in Adelaide for about three weeks, it was time to go home and try and get into the old routine again. Because the swelling took a while to go down, somebody made the comment to mum that my face didn't look much different, and I wasn't too impressed. The following February I had to have the last operation on my nose to fully clear the airway. I was most likely the youngest patient in the Royal Adelaide Hospital, and guess where they put me? In with a group of old ladies, so there was certainly not a lot of activity in the ward. Every day at 2pm it was time to have a sleep. The blinds would all be shut for a couple of hours until visiting hours started. One of the things that came out of all of the tests was that I didn't need to use contact lenses anymore, so I could now officially throw them on the rubbish dump. The eye specialist couldn't work out why I had been given them to start with as they had become too strong for me. Most days when I had been going to school I would go to the toilets and take them out because I knew that mum would check the containers at home. It was at this stage of my life that I decided what I wanted in return for all that I had been through. Only one thing and that was a child of my own. I didn't want a lot of money and material things as they don't make you happy, I already knew from experience. I am not real sure why I chose this, maybe I felt that if I was granted my wish that nobody would be able to take it away from me and I would be able to give a child all the love and attention that I never had from my own parents. I knew that if I never married I would not be grant my wish, but that never bothered me at all. I believe that a child should start out life with two loving parents. I think I was also using my ability to have a child as a sense of security and felt that nobody could take it away from me. In 1980 mum took me to meet my paternal grandparents, I don't remember exactly how we found out where they were, but finally we got there. They were certainly not the type of people that I had expected and in some ways hoped for. For some reason I thought that they might be more outgoing, instead they were pretty quiet. I liked my Grandmother almost instantly as she seemed to be quite a nice lady. As far as my father's father went, right from the start I felt that he had something to hide because in my opinion he wasn't open enough. He seemed to act as if he was guilty of something. They were not much taller than me, so at least I had some idea of where I had inherited my height from. Granny had short wavy brown hair and Grandpa was going grey and balding. He also had glasses that looked as through he had worn them for the last 20 years. He seemed to have a lot of things going though his mind and every time we would visit he would be drinking beer, which I was not comfortable with. He also got on well with mum which I was please with and would tell her she was doing the right thing. Over a period of time I found out more about grandpa's personality, when mum and I would visito once or twice a year from Kangaroo Island. I found a lot of things about Grandfather which gave me an insight as to why my father might have been the way he was. It seemed that when my father, Barry, was a child, his father went off to war and he came back a different man, which in itself is understandable enough, but surely he would have made an attempt to catch up on lost time with his children. I know Barry did a lot of stupid things, but surely as his father, grandpa could have tried to keep the communication lines open instead of hanging up the phone when his son was trying to talk to him.

In my grandfather's eyes, his daughter could do no wrong, even though she had now married three times. I used to visit mainly for the sake of grandma, as she was really nice to me and she always had biscuits and a drink. Sometimes I would have lunch with them because I thought that they would appreciate my visits after all the years that they had missed out on. Eventually I learned just how much grandpa despised my other grandparents. It seems that even at the wedding they only spoke to each other briefly and after that there was not a lot of contact between them. This became very obvious to me when grandpa told me that he went into a butcher shop one day and there was my mother's father serving behind the counter. Instead of making himself known and saying hello etc. he just ignored him and carried on as if he never knew him at all. I thought to myself, how arrogant can you get, as after all, they shared the same grandchildren and surely that was a good enough reason to keep in contact, even if my parents' marriage had broken down. I really feel it's sad when one child is favoured over the other. Aren't you meant to treat your children as equals?

Something that will always interest me is the little book that grandpa had. He used to tell me different things out of it, but for some strange reason, he would not let me look at it by myself. I did however find out that there was a convict in our family tree, so I thought to myself hey! Not everyone has a convict in their family.

I had now been living on the island for thirteen years, so I knew a lot of people there and mum was related to most of them in some way or another, as she had married into quite a large family. When the population is only around four thousand people, is doesn't take very long to get to know quite a few. By this stage I had acquired quite a few special friends for whom I will always have a lot of respect. They were always there when I needed to talk when things were not going too well with Mum, because even though she was great in her role as a mother, I couldn't handle her strong views on certain things and I sometimes felt very restricted. I wished that I could leave and get away from it all. I lost count of the number of times that I went to bed and cried myself to sleep. I didn't know what to do because she was my only parent, and according to her, I wasn't to tell anybody about what was going on in our home. It was stupid little things, like I remember one day when I had just had my long hair trimmed for the first time in years, simply because mum did not believe in cutting it, and she cracked a fit. As punishment I had to have it up in a bun for a whole week. Also, I wasn't allowed to use perfume as it might attract boys! I remember mum would go through my drawers and take out anything she thought that I shouldn't have, even if it was given to me as a present. It didn't matter who gave it to me, or what it was, if it was in her mind that it had to go, then it did. She even threw out the perfume that Darryl had given me, and when it didn't explode in the incinerator, she decided she would bring it back inside and use it as a toilet freshener. To this day, Mum has no idea how I felt inside about this, as to me the perfume was very valuable, not because of what it was, but because of what it represented—that it was a gift from one of my real brothers who I was only just getting to know after not knowing that I even had any real family. It upsets me greatly that this thought did not cross my Mum's mind.

Another time she decided to throw out my tampons because she had the strange idea that they just might (in her words) turn me on! I couldn't believe what I was hearing as her excuse, and what made it worse was the fact that this happened just before my period was due and I didn't earn a lot of money to run out and replace them. I had to keep reminding her that you can't make a teenager see things in the same way as a person in the fifties or sixties.

One night it all came to a head and I knew that I had just had enough of mum's insistence regarding how long I said my prayers for, and just how long I would read my bible at night. This particular night, mum had walked into my room and turned on the light when I was just about asleep and demanded that I read the bible a bit longer and also say my prayers for a bit longer as well. So I picked up the bible and threw it across the room at her so she would get the message that I had had enough of her interference. I had almost gotten to breaking point, the point where I didn't care if I never read the bible again, even though I believed in it. I know a lot of the time this problem did put a strain on our relationship to the stage where mum said that if I wasn't willing to follow the rules, I would have to leave. I would have packed up then and left, if I'd had somewhere to go. I didn't want to lose the family that I had grown to love as my own, so I was sort of stuck and I just had to ride it out and hope that one day I would get an opportunity to leave the island, even though I loved living there. At the same time Mum could be described as being witty—she had a great sense of humour to the point where sometimes we would laugh at each other, simply because our eyes met at a humorous moment, which was good as it helped break any tension. She was also very caring and determined in the things she chose to do and would not give up very easily, thank goodness as this attitude was to serve her well when I entered her life. What a brave lady!

A lot of things happened at home that never should have, but I'm not going to put them down in writing, because I know it would hurt some of my best and closest friends, and that is NOT the reason why I have chosen to write about my life.

I found it very hard to express my own personality without the fear of being controlled by mum, so I just ended up going with the flow so to speak, just to keep the peace at home. I was always pleased when visitors came, as it gave me a break in what had become a very, very strict code of living. It wasn't that I wanted to do anything stupid such as smoke, take drugs or even have sex before marriage, I just wanted to be a normal teenager and young adult, without having someone control my every move. As a result of having to live by mum's rules, I soon learned how to be sneaky and do a lot of things that to this day she doesn't know about, just so I could survive emotionally.

It was during this period of time that I just wished that I had a father, because I knew that I would have someone to talk to who would most likely have a different point of view to mum. I would often talk to my friends who I felt that I could trust, I had to talk to somebody, otherwise I would have gone around the twist. A person can't continue to live in this type of environment without it having an effect. Apart from this, we did have a lot of good times together. A week before I left the island, I was taken out for lunch at the Country Harvest in the main street of Kingscote by a group of my friends. They will always be special to me as we shared a lot of good times together, even though they were at least ten years older then me. We would often go to Emu Bay in the summer months for swimming and fishing with nets and finish the evening off with a huge bonfire. In the winter months, I would often be invited to a pot luck tea which was really enjoyable, as you never knew what there would be to eat because everybody would take a different dish.

The year before I left home had to be one of the worst years of my young adult life so far. I found out that I only had one good fallopian tube left, thanks to somebody not doing their job thoroughly enough. I had been going to the doctor because of persistent pain on my right side, only to be told that it was the way I was going to the toilet, meaning my bowels were not working properly. Personally I couldn't work out what was wrong with them, as I hadn't noticed anything, but I believed what the doctor said and I was given this gluggie stuff to take every day. Things didn't appear to change so I kept on going back to the same doctor, and that would turn out to be my biggest mistake. But how was I to know? I thought that it made sense and that the doctor would know what was going on, because generally I was a healthy person.

It was very frustrating, as I was now becoming aware of being able to feel something in the lower part of my abdomen. I couldn't seem to make the doctor understand or else he wasn't asking the right questions. I eventually gave up going because I felt that I was getting nowhere and mum was saying that it was all in my mind. That didn't help either. This continued to go on for what seemed to be the best part of a year until the long weekend of Easter, when I had intended to go to Adelaide for the weekend. For some reason, which I'm not quite sure about, I changed my mind.

I woke up on the Friday morning not feeling one hundred percent but I didn't take a lot of notice as I was getting used to the pain and with the doctor not doing anything to find out what the cause was and I was fast losing faith in the medical profession. Gradually as the day went on, the pain got worse so I decided that if it was still bad the next day, I would go to the outpatients department if I couldn't get a regular appointment. I never made it to the next day. When I went to bed at ten pm, the pain was still going only by now I had no breaks in between sessions. Now I was just hoping that I could make it until the morning. My morning started a lot earlier than normal. I woke at 1am to find myself doubled up with pain. It was now obvious to me that something was very wrong and the pain had gotten to the point of being almost unbearable. I knew that I had to wake up mum as I needed help. By this time I was all bent over and unable to stand up straight at all. I couldn't even sit because I couldn't stand any pressure on the lower part of my body. I had already been to the toilet and I felt like I had to throw up but nothing happened. The problem was definitely in my stomach area.

After getting back to the lounge room where mum was on the telephone to the hospital, I somehow ended up under the table curled up like an unborn child and just at that moment, one of the visitors who was staying with us at the time, happened to come to see what was going on and asked me if I was looking for something underneath the table. I thought to myself, what a stupid question, why would a person get up at this time of the night, just to check the floor! By the time I got to the hospital, my hearing had become very distant and my sight had become blurry, strangely enough though, I wasn't feeling sick in the stomach anymore, so at least I had something to be grateful for. I just happened to get the same doctor who I had already seen regarding my persistent problem. I thought to myself that surely this time he would find out what was going on. My fingers had gone limp and my stomach was now as hard as a rock. I think it was nature's way of protecting it. A check was done to see if I had appendicitis maybe that has the same symptoms as what I had—who knows! I felt really bad getting the doctor out of bed at that hour of the night, but then again, it's their chosen job so I guess they expect it to happen. I was given a needle to stop the nausea and pain, even though I didn't feel sick anymore, but I was too sick to tell them that I didn't need it. I spent the next day in hospital just waiting to see if anything else would happen, but nothing did. The doctor didn't even spend any time with me asking what had happened the day before. This would have given him a good idea of what went horribly wrong. My aunty called in to see me and one of her comments was "you don't look sick". Boy oh boy, I thought to myself, if only you had seen me last night you wouldn't be saying that and even mum (who by now had become a bit of hard case in regards to me going to the doctor all of the time because of my stomach problems), didn't appreciate her comment. walked home from the hospital on the Sunday morning because nothing was happening and even though I felt a bit off, I didn't have the pain that I had been experiencing in the past. I never bothered to go back to see what, or if anything, could be done, or to find out what had happened because there were no blood tests or anything done.

Things were fine for the next couple of weeks, until I started to get all cold and shivery, and yet I felt hot at the same time. I was at my friend's house, and she said to me "Debbie, you're not going to get sick on me are you?" I suppose I should have gone to see the other doctor to find out what was going on, but I simply couldn't see the point as nothing had been done before, so why would they do something now?

I could not believe my luck as now the pain had started again, but this time it was occurring every day for period ranging from five minutes up to 30 minutes without a break. The best way I can describe it is that it felt as if something was pulling. I started going back to the doctor with the hope that this time he would find out what on earth as going on. I was starting to wonder if it was all in my mind because nobody was doing anything about it. This sort of experience doesn't do anything for your self-esteem, and you slowly lose confidence in yourself. Also, what was making it worse was the fact that mum was telling me that it was my imagination and that the doctor was only giving me fake medicine. I really began to wonder how someone can be so heartless. Generally I never got sick, so why on earth would I be making the whole thing up? Fortunately I changed doctors as I have given up on the first one, for obvious reasons. At least this time I was given tablets to take, because he thought that maybe there was something wrong with my bowel.

After it was apparent that the medication wasn't having any effect, I insisted on seeing a Gynaecologist. One of my friends suggested to me that I might have a problem in that area, and I thought I should at least rule out that possibility. The female doctor was not too bad in my eyes, until one day she told me off for tensing up during a pelvic examination. I was scared stiff of what she was going to do, after all, I had never had an examination like that before; it was all new to me. I was to told I would have to have an operation called a laparoscopy to try and find out what was going on inside.

The private hospital was nice, but I was scared and yet relieved at the same time. At least now, something was being done, so I wasn't going to complain. The wound was not as sore as I had expected, but I was sorer on the inside than I thought I would be. It wasn't very nice when I came to. I felt freezing cold and wanted an extra blanket, but I couldn't ask for one because I couldn't talk or move. Finally, the morning came and I waited for the doctor to walk in the room and have a decent chat, but that didn't happen. Instead, the phone next to my bed rang, and it was the lady doctor. I don't know why she never bothered to see me in person, but maybe that's the way she was. I never expected to hear what she was about to tell me, as it was the furthest thing from my mind. She was just very straight to the point, and briefly explained that my right fallopian tube was twisted and stuck to my bowel, as a result of having an ovarian cyst burst, but it was alright because I still had one good one!

Later that day I went back to my friend's house where I stayed until I could return to the Island following my check-up and having my stitches removed. By the time I arrived home I was a total emotional wreck as I had used the fact that there was nothing wrong with my reproductive organs as my sense of security, and my ticket to being granted my only wish in life, and now even that was threatened.

A few of my friends mentioned to me that my eyes looked as if something was wrong with them, but I didn't realise the possible connection between that and the fact that I wasn't feeling very good, even though I had felt something was wrong when I first woke up from the operation. I know now, that I should have gone to see the doctor, but as I have already mentioned, I was in total shock and I couldn't stand the thought of seeing yet another doctor so soon. I felt totally lost and upset and I was crying when I was doing the dishes, which I could hardly see I can remember mum saying that I shouldn't be angry at the doctor and I thought to myself why the hell not? I couldn't believe how this could have happened. But everything was falling into place, and the sequence of events on the long weekend made sense. It will always be beyond me how on earth a doctor could be so careless, as after all, it should have been very clear that something had gone terribly wrong. Maybe if I had been able to scream, I would have received a lot better treatment, but I couldn't because when I'm in a lot of pain, I go very quiet I honestly believe that if the pain had been any worse I would have lost consciousness. I mentioned earlier that my vision had gone blurry, and my hearing was very distant. I am only too thankful that it did not turn out to be an undetected cancer, as I'm sure if that had been, I wouldn't be here writing about it now.

I finally left the Island in June of 1987. I needed to find some decent work, and jobs were very limited on the Island and I was only getting employment for six months of the year, working at Safcol during cray season. The rest of the time I would do a bit of baby sitting, which was really good as I got a lot of experience with children of different ages. Some of my friends had enquired around and found out that there was work for the next six months in a town about 200kms from Adelaide, so I went packing oranges until December. While I was working at the shed as it was known, I met a lot of nice people and I soon gathered myself another small group of genuine friends. Some days we would kill ourselves laughing and the time seemed to pass very quickly which was great, because it can become a bit monotonous when you do the same thing all day long. I decided during this time that I would find out whether or not I could have my right thumb straightened, which was supposed to have been done before now.

So, off I went to a highly recommended specialist to find out what was involved. What had to be done was the middle joint would be removed and it would be replaced with a pin. It didn't sound too bad to start with, but the more I thought about it, the less I liked the idea. It would make my thumb shorter than normal, and I would lose the mobility of it, and I knew that would be something I would miss because the fact it would now bend to accommodate what I was doing, made things easier. I think that nature is truly amazing, the way it has the ability to allow the body to adapt to make up for shortcomings in some areas. It's something that shouldn't be taken for granted. I believe that the human body is the best computer there is, and man, with all of his wisdom, can't match it.

During this time, I boarded with one of my mum's friend's daughters.

Mum had known the mother for years, and the daughter and I soon became good friends. We had a lot in common even though there was quite a difference in our ages. It was during this time that I met my future husband.

I was visiting another family one evening, and Ian was there, trying to sell some health products. I didn't even know Ian's last name, and I really didn't care either. I'm not sure how long it took for us to become best friends, but I knew that there was something different about him that was attracting me to him. As time went by, he became very special to me, and I said to one of my work mates that I was going to marry him one day. We used to spend a lot of time in the evenings down on the riverfront where we could be alone if we wanted to be. Mum had met Ian by now, and she didn't dislike him, but at the same time she was not encouraging me to keep the relationship going either. She was trying to push her opinion on to me yet again, and didn't want me to marry him. In her eyes, he didn't understand the Bible the same way she did.

Mum shouldn't have said anything, because she had done the same thing. I truly believe one thing in life, and that is if someone respects and loves you for who you are, you don't have the right to play God and judge them.

Christmas morning 1987, had been a laugh as I knew that Ian was an early riser, but I never expected to hear a knock on my bedroom window at six am! Here he was with a bunch of flowers and a present. It made my heart melt. I had never expected it and after all, Ian was my first boyfriend. Ian asked me if I would go to Queensland with him to meet his family, but I said no. I felt that the relationship was doomed because I wasn't strong enough to go against the opposition from my mother.

Apart from Ian, there was really nothing to keep me where I was, the work at the packing shed had run out and I felt that I would have a better chance of getting employment in Adelaide. Ian was not a city boy though, so there was no way that he would move to Adelaide, but I felt that I needed to go. I went down to see some friends in Victor Harbour for a few weeks before going up to the city. I really hated the idea of being unemployed because it did nothing for my self-esteem and people can really put you down, even if you've been trying to get work. I can remember very clearly one night when my friends had visitors down at Victor Harbour and one the guests, who should have known better, was just pulling me to pieces in front of everybody, regardless of the fact that I had been working for the last six months and I was still trying to get a job. What really upset me was the fact that nobody told him to shut up. It's not even manners to talk for the whole evening when you are a guest of someone else, let alone pick on someone. As a result of that evening, I felt like a total piece of junk and that I was worth nothing.

It was about this time that I decided to try and find out about my relations on mum's side of the family. I had already met my father's people, so I set about getting my mum's parents' marriage certificate and this told me how many children there were. My paternal grandparents had mentioned to me that they thought my mother's parents had both died in the 1970s, so I thought to myself, that's great! What am I going to do now? Just before this, Peter's wife had been writing to all the people who had the same surname in the phone book, and as it turned out my dad's parents were right—all the letters were returned or led to dead ends. I had been told that my maternal grandparents had lived in Tailem Bend for years, and might have been there at the time of their deaths. One day I went to visit the town, having never been there before, because I wanted to check out the street where my parents were supposed to have lived during their time there. I found out that they lived on the main road, and went there to check it out, thinking I might just find somebody to talk to who knew them. Before this though, I had been to the council office to check if they had records that my grandparents were buried in the cemetery there, and sure enough, I hit the jackpot. When the office girl told me what I was hoping to hear, I just said to her no wonder we couldn't find them in the phone book, and we both just laughed. I guess it sounded quite funny, considering what I had just told her about my past—I told her so she would understand why I needed her help. Anyhow, at least now I had somewhere to start.

I was told how to get to the cemetery and I had a rough idea of where the grave was but I thought to myself, knowing my luck, I would only find an unmarked grave. It was very important to me that this was not the case, as all I knew so far was that my grandfather had two children marked on his death certificate, and his wife had three children marked on hers.

Well, today my luck held out and sure enough, I found a really nice black marble headstone with a gold inscription on it. Even though I didn't know any of the family yet, I did feel sorry for them as it must have been very hard losing your parents so close together; there was less than eighteen months between their deaths. There was no-one around, so it really didn't matter how long I spent there. I sat down on the marble slab, and wondered what might have been. I had no idea what they might have looked like or under what circumstances they had lived or died. At least now though, I had a starting point so I was happy. I did feel sad because these were grandparents I had never known, and they passed away without ever knowing what happened to their grandchildren, something they didn't ask for. I was to later find out that my grandmother had died of a massive coronary in Tailem Bend Hospital, and my grandfather had died of cancer which had started in his kidneys. He passed away in Meningie Hospital. Until then, I never knew whether they had sons or daughters, but now I had my answers, so I just had to find out who they had married and where they were living. After taking a photo of the grave site and writing down the business name of the people who erected the monument, I went on to my next move.

On my way back I found the place in Murray Bridge where the monument had been made, and explained why I needed to know who had paid for it. They were very nice, but could only tell me that it was paid for out of the estate. Then I thought of a really good question, who was the undertaker? And yes—they did have the answer, a company by the name of GS and RS Minge and Sons of Murray Bridge. I thanked them very much, and went on my way. I was really very pleased with the way things were progressing in such a short time.

I decided to phone Mr Minge to see if he had any information about the family, and explain where I came into the picture. He was very nice, and as helpful as he could be, but apparently any information that the funeral directors get about the family is provided on a voluntary basis and as a result only the first names of the children were recorded along with their ages. Just before I hung up, I had another brilliant thought and I asked him if he knew the name of the company where the wills were being held. I knew that the children's full names would have to be stated correctly in the Will, and a Will has to be kept for quite some time after the estate has been wound up. Mr Minge gave me the name of the solicitor. When I rang them, their response was quite different from the other people I had spoken to. I guess it was because it's not normal for somebody to enquire about a Will eleven years after it has been executed. I had to explain very clearly that I wasn't after money or anything else from the estate, I just wanted to know the full names of the people mentioned in the Will so I could find my relatives. After getting this point across to the solicitor, he was quite nice and said to call back a week later when they would have the information ready for me.

The week seemed to go past very slowly, and I was wondering what I would find out when I called back. When I rang, the receptionist answered and got the information I was after. She said that it only mentioned my youngest Aunt. Without thinking too much, I said in a joking manner, "she's the one I want to know!" and we both laughed. I felt that in the middle of all this serious stuff, it was important to try and keep a sense of humour otherwise it would get to me. After all, it's wasn't really nice to go through this type of experiences as it made me feel very lonely. Not many people would understand what was going through my mind.

When I got home from the cemetery trip I told one of my close friends that I had gone to visit my grandparents, and she asked me how they were and I told her I didn't know because the wouldn't talk to me or let me in and I just had to sit outside. She didn't think too much of my grandparents and thought they were very rude, she hadn't ticked to the truth—that I had visited them in the cemetery. I just about killed myself laughing when I saw the expression on her face when I finally told her where I'd been.

It was only 1988, and I was beginning to feel as if I had achieved a lot in a very short time when often things like this can take years. As soon as I had another opportunity, I went to a house on the main highway, hoping to find someone who might have known my grandparents, and I was in luck yet again. I met a person who sent me further down the road to a couple, who appeared to be about the same age as my parents. I had to explain myself pretty well so they knew why I wanted to get in contact with anybody who might have known my Mother's parents. Little did I know that they also knew my father well and we spent quite a while talking about my grandparents etc. Finally I was sent down to see another old couple called Mr and Mrs Lee. They, it turned out, were two of my grandmother's closest friends and they still kept in contact with my youngest Aunty.

These old folks were very, very nice to me and we spent the rest of the afternoon talking together and finally things were falling into place. I discovered just how small this world could be as these people knew a lot I would not have found out from any other source. While I was at their house, they rang my Aunty to enquire how things were going, so I would have some idea of what to expect when I contacted her. Sadly I also found out just how many lies can be concealed under cemetery headstones, regardless of the wording and how elaborate they may be. The Lees had been friends with my grandparents for many years, so I learned a lot in the short time I was with them.

Apparently my grandmother had to be careful of what she did so she would not upset my grandfather. It seems that the day my mother turned me over to the Welfare, she had given her mother no warning about her plan, she just said to her "I gave Debbie away today." Regardless of what she thought of her mother, as my grandparent she surely had the right to know what was going to happen to me, even if only to say goodbye and whether or not she was to be part of any future plans? I do believe in my heart, that she should have been given the opportunity to say goodbye to me. It seems that she never really adjusted to not seeing me again, which is quite sad and I don't believe that my own mother had a right to do that to her.

Part of me was now happy that I wasn't kept with the family. Previously, I had always wondered why on earth they, as a unit, didn't try to keep me with them, but I now realised that it was my mother who felt that she didn't have many options open to her. As far as my feelings were now concerned, part of me was excited that finally I was finding the other half of my biological family, and another part of me was wondering "what have I done now?"

Mrs and Mr Lee

It was nearly December before I plucked up the courage to get in contact with my newly found Aunty. This was extremely draining on an emotional level as I had no idea what her reaction would be. I just had to hope for the best. After finding her phone number, I said to myself I couldn't chicken out now as I was so close to finding my Mother's family and I had put a lot of time and effort into tracing them. By now it was nearly Christmas, and a lot of people at this time of year are wondering what surprises will be waiting for them under the tree. I was just wondering what the outcome of the phone call I knew I had to make, would be, and so were my brother Peter and his wife after I told them what I'd found out so far.

I rang during the evening hours as I thought that would be the best time to catch my Aunty at home. Dialling the number was the easiest part of the whole thing. Finally the phone was answered and I guessed it was my Uncle. I think he asked me who was speaking, so I just said it was Debbie, his wife's niece, and could I please speak to her. He was away from the phone for what seemed like an eternity, and then finally I heard my Auntie's voice. I really didn't know what to say. I had no idea what her reaction would be and it felt like I was almost in another world where I had absolutely no idea of what would happen next. I did feel a bit sorry for her because she had no warning that anything like this was going to happen and it must have come as somewhat of a shock, especially as they had been lead to believe I had died years earlier. It was certainly different to when I met Peter and Darryl for the first time. This time I had to come to grips with an older generation.

My Aunty decided that I could come down to Meningie to meet her on Boxing Day. It felt like one of the longest drives that I had ever been on. Apart from the fact I had never been to Meningie before and it was a stinking hot day, I really didn't know what to expect when I arrived. The town itself wasn't really that big, and was situated on Lake Alexandrina. I knew what street they lived in, but had no idea of the house number so I had to call in and ask somebody to tell me where my Aunt and Uncle lived. I pulled into a house and knocked on the door. An elderly lady answered and I just said to her "could you please tell me where Mr and

Mrs * * * live?" To my surprise, she said "oh, you must be the girl that was given away by your Mother." I thought to myself, does everyone in this town know about me? After she told me where they lived, I said thank you and followed her directions to the house. By now I was starting to feel the same way I did when I met the boys for the first time. I went around to the back door and knocked, not knowing if they had seen me out of the window. Now I just had to wait as I had no idea of what these people looked like, or how they would react when they saw me. The waiting was over and it was my uncle who came to the door and asked me to come in. I went into the kitchen and waited for my aunty who was in another part of the house. I don't know how my aunty was feeling, but all I can say for myself is that I was wondering what was going to be said. It wasn't like in the movies where everyone gets a hug and carries on as if you had met each other years before and you just sit down and take up where you left off. They just stood there looking at me and saying things like "doesn't she look like her father?", or "doesn't she look like her mother?" It made me feel like a baby being admired for the first time by the whole family. At this stage, I had no idea what my mother looked like, let alone my father. I was invited to stay for lunch and I met most of my cousins. I did spend a lot of time just looking at them all and thinking to myself, do these people really belong to me? They were all very nice to me and after they had all left, family photos came out. They were very interesting to me as I could see where I got my looks from. I was even given a few to keep and pass on to Peter if I wanted to. Finally it was time to go back to Adelaide after what had been an emotionally draining day, and I was actually glad it was over.

When I first arrived in Adelaide I had to stay with one of my foster aunties for a few weeks until I could find somewhere else to stay. I couldn't believe my luck (or lack of it), when I found myself having to stay at the home of the person who had pulled me to pieces at Victor Harbour. At this stage I really didn't have anywhere else to go and I really didn't want to stay at a boarding house or worse still, go back to Kangaroo Island and live with mum again, so I stayed. Most days weren't too bad, their daughter had become one of my best friends and we had a lot of laughs together, apart from the fact that the tension between family members would get very intense sometimes. It made me feel sick in the stomach and scared stiff of what was going to happen next. There were six of us living in one house. My one big lesson out of it all was that I should never become too involved with anyone as I found myself becoming the meat in a sandwich, even if I'd done nothing, or had nothing to do with a situation.

Finally, I was getting lucky. I applied for a position working in a smallgoods factory which was run in conjunction with Woolworths, and I was accepted. At this stage Ian was still writing to me and visiting as well, but the relationship was not as good as it could have been. I was coming to the realisation I had to give him up because I didn't feel emotionally strong enough to go against mum's wishes and what others were trying to tell me to do. Even though I loved him, I was getting frustrated by the whole situation. I wanted to do one thing, but others wanted me to take their advice, so I finally just chucked in our relationship and hoped that Ian would understand.

I stayed at my new job for the next three years and I'm sure that I packed every type of cold meat there is during that period of time. Some of my work mates were really funny and we had a few good laughs, talking about any topic ranging from doughnuts, to what we thought of the male of our species. Fred, who was a bachelor, was tops and he could come up with a stupid remark at the least expected times, and Helen, Kylie and I would kill ourselves laughing. Alvin was another one who would always have something to say without fail. I couldn't help but smile and then he would say "what are you looking at?" His wife Dot was quite a nice person underneath her rock hard exterior, but I felt that she took her job far too seriously. Then again, that wouldn't be too hard when you're working in the same room as the boss who was as dull as the cement surface on the back verandah. I always tried to keep my mouth shut so I wouldn't get myself into trouble. For some reason, the factory went through casual employees like I went through toilet paper. I lost count of just how many came and went in the three years I was there. By the end of the second year I was getting to the stage of almost having had enough. I hadn't had a decent break and a person can't work indefinitely. Sometimes when things were not going the way management thought they should, I could feel the tension and it was not unusual to see Dot watching everything from her office window. It wasn't a very pleasant atmosphere to work in. I believed the main problem was most likely the fact that the people who were meant to be running it had been there too long and could no longer tell the difference between running the place and being a group of dictators who had no (or very little) respect for the people out on the floor. If you weren't in their favour, you could lose out big time so you had to watch your back. Some might not agree with my observations, but that's how I saw it. Fortunately, I managed to keep my head above water and not rattle anyone's cage too much, and keep myself in a job that I couldn't afford to lose.

Karen, Peter and me—1989

I was living in a nice flat at Glenside. I used to pack all types of cold meat all day and generally got about eight hours work a day, sometimes in the summer we could get anything up to ten or twelve hours. Doing the same job day after day didn't really bother me, I was happy just to be earning my own money instead of being on the dole. It's beyond me why some people have no desire to work when the dole money is only just enough to keep you afloat, even if you spend it wisely.

I had been working at my job for over two years when I went into the office and asked Dot if I could have some time off so I could go to Queensland to meet my sister for the first time. She didn't want to let me go, but I stuck up for myself and told her exactly what I needed to do. You should have seen her face when I told her I'd never met my sister before. Her face went bright red and her mouth dropped open. I was planning on going for three weeks. I flew up to Brisbane where I was picked up by Peter, who drove me to the bus station. I was going by bus to Mackay to stay with parents of my friends for about ten days. The bus trip was very tiring so I slept most of the day after I arrived. Then I made my own way down to Brisbane, where I would meet Karen for the first time. I was very excited at the prospect of meeting her; I couldn't believe I would finally have a sister of my very own. Karen came out to Dalby to meet me and I thought that we hit it off very well, considering we didn't know each other at all. I had arranged to have some professional photographs taken to mark the occasion, because for the first time in our whole lives, the three of us would be together. The photos turned out great so it was well worth the expense. Karen is slightly taller than me and also has a figure I could only dream of.

When we got talking, the picture seemed to get clearer in some ways, but foggier in others. Karen had been brought up as an only child, not knowing about the rest of us. It's totally beyond me why my Mother thought that she had the right to deny Karen the knowledge that she had other family, even though she might not ever meet them. Well now the past and all of the omissions were catching up with her, and she had nowhere to hide. I thought to myself how true it is that you can run, but you can't hide. In this case, my Mother had to face up to her past, regardless of how painful it might be. Peter had asked me if I would like to see my Mum, and I said I would be willing to see her on the condition that if she didn't take the opportunity this time while I was up there, she would never get another chance. Before this I had taken Karen and her two boys (Timothy and Adam) to Sea World. I thought this would help us relax a bit because meeting your family for the first time in these circumstances is not an experience I would wish on anyone. We had a great time together and later that night we went out on the train to have a look around Brisbane. As I had gone into Brisbane with Karen, I slept at her place for two or three nights. I was to leave on the Sunday to come home, and Saturday was the day Peter had arranged to pick up our Mother to come and see me. It was hard enough trying to get to know my sister, as well as knowing that I would soon see my Mother for the first time, and possibly the last time. Peter for some reason, had gotten a bit protective of our Mother, to the point of telling me to be careful of what I said to her in case it sent her blood pressure up. I just simply said to him "what about what she's done to us?" I didn't feel that I should pussyfoot around her just because I'd never seen her for all these years.

After all, did I owe her anything? I don't think so!

Peter went to Tweed Heads where our Mother and her third husband lived in a Caravan Park. I did have some idea of what she might look like as my middle Aunty had shown me some photos of her when she married her second husband. He had legally adopted Karen when she was quite young, but sadly died of liver trouble not many years later. My Mother is quite a bit shorter than me and has a much fuller figure, so I don't think that I'm too bad after all. I was sitting on my bed nursing Karen's cat when I heard the car pull up, so I peeked out the window to see how she my Mother was acting. I know I was wishing I could just disappear.

They came inside and went to the kitchen, where they sat down and started talking about football. There was never a question from my Mother like "where's Debbie?" After all, I was the reason she had come to Karen's in the first place. I was trying to get used to hearing her voice, when Peter came to check on me and why I wasn't coming into the kitchen to say hello. I couldn't put it off any longer, so in I went. Earlier in the day, Karen had said to me that if I didn't feel comfortable I should say I had to go downstairs to get the washing off the line as an excuse to leave the room.

When I walked in, my Mother didn't seem to take too much notice of me and just continued to talk football, which I actually thought was a bit inappropriate considering what was happening. I looked at her and thought to myself, "Are you really the lady who gave me away?" I continued to look at her, but I couldn't speak. It's sort of hard to explain how I was feeling, but it was like there was nothing between us, just an emotional void.

My Mother only spoke to me three times in the two days she was there. She asked me how I was, and as you might understand, I lied and told her that I was alright and she also asked me where I lived and worked. I didn't mind, as I had said to Peter, if she wanted to become my friend I wouldn't stop her, but she would never be more to me than that. On the Saturday night we all went out to tea at Sizzlers, and I couldn't help myself when I saw just how much she was eating, and I blurted out "you've got a big appetite haven't you?" I don't know if I offended her, but I really didn't care. Just before we left Jenny's parents place to go to the airport, it was decided that we would take some photos out on the back lawn area. It was more like parkland than a back yard. I didn't mind having the photos taken, as long as I didn't have to stand near our Mother. She was no more than a stranger to me. When I got the photos back, it was easy to see that we three kids all had the same parents.

On the way to the airport Peter tried to tell me how to say goodbye to our Mother. I think that he thought there might be a small chance of all of us becoming closer. I didn't like him trying to tell me how to say goodbye to her as she was not in any way special to me, so I didn't see any point in giving her a nice farewell speech.

As time went on, things seemed to go on alright between the three of them and I thought to myself, we'll just make it. I lived in Adelaide, so I didn't have much contact with Karen let alone our Mother, but I would hear from Peter now and then how things were. Unfortunately this didn't last as somehow our Father got Karen's address. We think it must have been from Darryl. At that stage, Darryl was living in Western Australia and our Father had been in contact with him. Karen didn't want her father knowing where she was living as like me, she didn't know him, so Peter's time and effort had gone down the drain. Poor Peter, he got the blame for telling Barry, and I thought to myself if only Karen had used her brain, she would have realised that Peter wouldn't have been so stupid to do something that would undo what he tried so hard to pull together. Our Mother was no better either, instead of encouraging Karen to keep up her contact with Peter and me, which to me should have become more treasured with time, she didn't encourage her as we had done nothing wrong. To this day, we don't hear anymore from Karen or our Mother. I will never feel sorry for my Mother again, she had her chance and as far as I'm concerned, she will never be part of my life. Children are not like toys that you can put away in the cupboard when you are tired of them. Now I realise why the people in Tailem Bend said she was very immature.

Up until now I had continued my visits to my Paternal Grandparents, but it became apparent that this was causing problems for Granny every time I left. As I mentioned, Leo would get very agitated very quickly, and sit at the kitchen table drinking beer while we were in the lounge room chatting and having tea. I had no idea what it was about my visits that upset him so much so I just tried to ignore it. During my visits however, the subject of my Father would always seem to come up with Leo's help, and he never had anything good to say about him. I put up with this for quite a while but eventually I'd had enough as surely my Father must have had at least one good attribute. Finally they moved from Hyde Park into a smaller unit that would be easier for Granny to look after. By now they were both over seventy and when you're that age, you don't need a big house to look after, especially when you only use three rooms. I went to see them a few times at their new unit until one day it was very evident that I couldn't visit my Grandmother anymore because my Grandfather was taking whatever it was that was bothering him, out on Granny after I left, and I couldn't put her through that, it wasn't fair to her.

The last day I went to visit, I could feel the tension before I walked in, but I thought I won't be rude and turn away, especially as they could already see me coming down the footpath. As soon as Grandfather let me in, he said to Granny "give her cup of tea and just get rid of her as soon as possible." I looked at Granny and said to her "what on earth is wrong with him today?" I could tell by the look on her face that she didn't have the answer either. When the visit was nearly over we were out in the kitchen and suddenly he just stood up and let loose. He looked at me and told me in no uncertain terms to get out before he called the police. He was treating me like I had committed a crime and as far as I know my only crime was my very existence. By now he was very red in the face and I thought his blood pressure just might go through the roof causing him to have a stroke or something. What made him madder still was the fact that I wasn't scared of him, and I stood there acting as if nothing was wrong, thinking to myself "how stupid are you?" To this day, I have no idea what set him off, but I'm pretty sure that I can say he was so full of guilt that he couldn't stand the sight of me. It was very evident that he never went out of his way to help out with the Grandchildren when they needed it most.

When I got home I rang up his daughter, my Aunty, and told her what had happened. I was worried about leaving Granny because of what may have happened to her after I left. I told her I was going to write a letter telling him how disappointed I was in him, and she told me that she thought what happened had been coming for a long time. I couldn't believe it, but it was obvious that she felt the same way I did, so it was clear to me that this would have to be my last visit if Granny had to suffer after I'd been. I also felt that it wasn't fair to me to have been put in that situation, especially when I didn't know what was wrong, and it had taken a lot out of me to get used to the idea of finally visiting Grandparents I didn't know I had.

It was now I decided that I wanted out of my job, but the big problem was that I couldn't take time off work to go for interviews. If I had, I may well have lost my job in the process, because any prospective employer would want a reference from Chisholm's—my current employer. There was only one way to do it, and that was to wait until I was given some time off. Previously I had been speaking to one of my friends who had recently been working as a nanny in Canada, and as I loved children and wanted the chance to travel, I figured this was the perfect opportunity. I got in touch with a nanny agency in Newcastle, New South Wales. The lady who ran the agency was very helpful and agreed to let me come up for interview as soon as I could organise it. The chance to do that came in April 1990. At work we were all asked if anyone would like some time off, so I jumped at the opportunity. I was away for one week and in that time I managed to get to Newcastle. I caught a bus from Adelaide which travelled overnight and then connected with a train next morning. Later that day I arrived at the Sydney train terminal, and then caught another train onto Newcastle. I stayed in a hotel across from the train station. My interview had been arranged for the following morning, and it was within walking distance, so I saw a bit of the business area of the city.

I couldn't believe my luck! I passed the interview and paid the fee of $400.00 which covered the agency's time and bookwork. I knew that I would be going to Canada because I was past the cut off age to go to England, but it didn't matter as Mum had her two nieces and nephew and their father living in different parts of the country. I was over the moon as I had done it! Now the hardest part was keeping my mouth shut until I knew that I would definitely be going as I didn't want to lose my current job.

In October 1990 I received a job offer from a family In Calgary, Alberta. After thinking about their offer I accepted, only to find out they had changed their mind and decided to have a family member fill the position. It didn't really worry me because I knew it was only a matter of time until I received another offer. The second offer also came in October. It was from a family who had two boys, and they also lived in Calgary. After carefully considering their offer, I decided this was the family for me. Now we just had to get all the Immigration documents in order before I could get an airline ticket. I was really excited now, I had never been overseas and the thought of being in a 747 jumbo for over eleven hours didn't bother me in the least. A few people I knew couldn't understand why I was so confident that I should go through with this idea, but I guess when you think about it, I was heading into another of life's experiences.

When I finally told the folks at work that I was leaving and going overseas, they were totally shocked as they hadn't seen it coming. I was pleased with myself that I had managed to pull it off, so it was decided before I left that they would take me out to dinner at the Adelaide Casino and it turned out to be a blast. I can still hear poor Helen yelling from inside when I parked the car in front of her house before we went in to the City.

"Oh my God", she could not believe her eyes, as I had lost so much weight. I was now down to size 12 and she had no idea under our baggy factory clothes just how skinny I had become. I was given flowers and a watch which was really a surprise as I had no idea what they thought of me as a person and as a workmate. I then stayed with Mum for a few days before I left. It was quite tiring packing up all my belongings, but I planned to stay overseas for at least two years.

I finally left Adelaide Airport on 28th February, 1991, three months before my 30th birthday and to my total surprise, there were over 20 people there to see me off. By the time I had got to the end of the lineup I was nearly in tears. I had never thought that I meant much to these people and then when it sank in—what I was really doing.

Crossing the Pacific was another new experience for me and just the beginning of a whole new adventure which would end up lasting more than three years.

When I arrived in Calgary, Alberta it was 10pm, still on the 28th. I was very tired. I was picked up by the husband of my new family and I was to be introduced to the two boys aged seven and nine the next morning. That day was really full on, I had taken everyone Aussie souvenirs and the boys' mother took me shopping to get some suitable footwear as it was their winter. I feel that I successfully achieved a lot while I was with this family. I gained my Alberta Drivers Licence because I needed to be the boys' taxi to school and also take them to their playmates' homes etc. I had only been in Calgary for a couple of weeks when I got in contact with Mum's youngest Canadian niece who was really happy when I called. She didn't know I was coming over to work. I finally got to meet her and her family (lovely people), and we got on really well, so I spent quite a bit of time with them including Christmas which was very special.

I had only been with my new family for five months and we all went off to Florida to visit Disneyworld which is in Orlando. This trip was nothing short of fun, fun, fun. In the daytime hours we would take the children to the parks together as a family, and in the evenings I would catch the shuttle bus from the resort where we were staying to whichever Disney Park I wanted to go back to if I had not done all of the things I wanted during the day.

On the return trip while my new family stayed with relatives, I had the opportunity to stay with Mum's oldest Canadian niece and her family. They were very kind to me and they took me to visit Niagara Falls in New York State. This natural beauty could be watched for hours on end and it would always appear to be different. We went on a tour of the tunnels which lets you see the water spray drop in a vertical fashion and every part of you that isn't covered up with a rain-jacket is left totally soaked. The only thing we didn't get to do was go on the boat ride which takes you as near to the Falls as possible. The other trip we did was into Toronto, this we did by the Go train. We had dinner up in the C. N. Tower which is a revolving restaurant and takes about 90 minutes to be a full circle. The view was endless and watching the sunset just added to the magic of it all.

For a while now, with the encouragement of my new family, I had been thinking of going back to school to finish off high school. I decided that if there was any chance of me wanting to remain living in Canada, that it was the only thing to do—to get myself a proper career, and besides, it looks really good when you need to report to the Canadian Immigration Department for your yearly work visa. I was quite pleased with myself because I enrolled in the Adult Learning system which was running classes several hours a week and that allowed me to catch up on the basics. I would drop the boys off at school in the morning and then go to my own classes, after which I would go home and do my set chores to keep the home running. It didn't take too long for me to make progress, and I made remarkable improvements in the areas of maths and also English. I made a big decision now that I wanted to become a criminologist as this was the type of work had fascinated me for as long as I could recall. I was prepared to do whatever it took because I knew that it would not be too long before I would be given permission to stay in Canada and become a permanent resident. My plan was going great until the boys' mother lost her permanent employment and it wasn't feasible for me to stay with the family, so it was time to move on.

I didn't take very long at all to find another position as a nanny, however this meant I could no longer continue with my education which was a shame, but could not be helped. I was now looking after another little boy who was only 4 months old and it was agreed that I would also mind another little boy who was 10 weeks older. I felt that I managed them very well; they were actually a bit like twins.

In the second year I was with my new family, I took on a new charge instead of the first extra child, because his family didn't need my child minding services anymore. The boys and I had a great routine going, including watching Sesame Street first thing in the morning which allowed me time to do the tidying up and the chores and then we would go for a walk. By the time we arrived back home it would be sleep time before lunch. I met a couple of other Nannies and sometimes we got together so the boys could play. My new family was Jewish so I learnt a bit about their beliefs. Nothing like a new global experience in the journey of life!!

While I was still with my first family I had been asked if I ever had a boyfriend. I told them what had happened and they suggested that I write to Ian. I did and we began writing to each other again. One time I wrote and asked him if he would come over for a holiday, never thinking that he would turn up. Well, to my surprise that's exactly what happened!

Ian arrived when I had just returned from an amazing four day cruise to the Bahamas which is just off the east coast of Florida. I also spent five days in Miami in a lovely hotel overlooking the coastline. Part of the holiday package included car rental and that allowed me to drive to Cape Canaveral where the Kennedy Space Centre (normally known as NASA) is located. The two hour bus tour was truly inspiring from an engineering point of view and those of us who didn't understand the technical terms still found it breathtaking what man has managed to achieve in his quest to get to the moon.

I had big plans of driving back to Florida Keys the day before I was due to leave but I only managed to get 90 minutes down the road and the fanbelt on the rental car snapped, so I spent the next four hours on the side of the road watching the traffic pass by before the tow truck came to change over the car for me. I have to admit that I was not impressed with the fact that on several occasions the police drove by and didn't even bother to stop to check if I was alright, after all I was by myself on this four lane highway in a foreign country. Apart from this small hiccup I did enjoy myself and I did take some great photos so I won't forget that trip in a hurry.

Unbeknown to be me, Ian had been telling people that he was going to marry me. Ian spent about six weeks in Canada and most of the time he was doing the tourist thing, going places on the buses. I did manage to get some time off so we hired a car and I took him to places like Jasper and we saw the Columbia Ice fields and we drove down to Lake Louise. I feel that I was very, very fortunate living in Calgary as it was only a 90 minute drive west to the Canadian Rockies which are truly breathtaking, something which I could never get tired of looking at. The special bonus of living with my second family was that it was right behind Mum's niece's home, just around the corner.

Engagement Photo

During Ian's trip in 1993 he proposed to me totally out of the blue. We were staying at a Log Cabin Resort near Jasper and after asking him a few very important questions, I very happily accepted his proposal. As you might imagine, I was over the moon because I have mentioned previously that I had only given him up due to pressure from others. I simply could not believe that I had actually got him back! The experience of being overseas had given me more self-confidence to make my own choices in life without caring about what others would say. We chose the wedding date and Ian and I went and picked out our wedding rings, which was so romantic, in all my life I never pictured myself doing this as to me it always seemed to happen to someone else.

By the time I was due to leave Canada, I had been there three and a half years and it had been a totally amazing experience to the point of making me think that if possible, every young person—before they settle down and get married, should do something like this as it opens your eyes in a lot of ways. I feel it's disappointing that people become so narrow-minded, because they miss out on so much.

So, now my time in Canada was up and even though I knew that it was not going to be easy leaving all my new friends, I was very excited at the thought of Ian and me getting married on the 16th of July, in just 10 days time.

I was driven to the airport by my cousin which whom I stayed for a few days after leaving my last family. A few of my new friends were there to see me off and it was really hard. One of the little boys I had looked after came to the airport with his family to see me off as he hadn't seen a plane before. He gave me a single red rose and when I picked him up to say goodbye, they told him I was going on the plane and he looked me straight in the eye and asked "how come"? It was nearly more than I could take as I had grown to love him in the past 12 months, the result of having a lot to do with him and his parents.

As my flight to Vancouver progressed I had very mixed feelings for obvious reasons. I was leaving what so far could only be described as one of the best experiences of my life and now I was returning home to what I could only hope would be a life time of experiences with my best friend and soon to be husband. The fact that we were actually getting married was a miracle in itself, because if I had never left Australia, I wouldn't have got Ian back into my life. I never realised that people could be so different and thank goodness everyone is not the same, because then what sort of world would it be?

By the time the jumbo reached Sydney I was very tired, picking up the time I had lost when I left for overseas more then three years ago. I had not had much rest during the trip as I spent most of my time watching the stowaway cupboard. I had placed my dress and fur jacket there. I couldn't afford to replace either item and there was no insurance available, travelling from one continent to another. When I reached Sydney I was supposed to place the rose in the bin, but I couldn't bring myself to do it so I decided to leave it in the cabin crew's office on the plane. I can only hope that whoever found it, it brought them some of the happiness that it brought me in the short time I had it with me.

Mum and Ian met me at Adelaide Airport and then we all went to Mum's unit, which until now I had only heard about. Mum moved there while I was overseas. I was in Adelaide for less than two days and in that time a few friends came to see me and give Ian and me some wedding presents, so now it was starting to sink in. It seemed to be a very long drive to reach Queensland when we left Adelaide late in the afternoon. We ended up trying to have a sleep in the back of Ian's ute which as far as I was concerned was impossible. I felt as if I was laying on bare bones. We were getting married in Dalby because I wanted to get married where my brother Peter and his wife and children could be with us because to me that would be very special.

Regardless of the upcoming wedding, I was starting to feel a bit nervous about meeting Ian's family. I had only spoken to his mother on the phone before I left Canada and it's very difficult to describe what it felt like being in this position. We went into Brisbane first to see Ian's sister and her family. I thought to myself that these don't seem bad people, yet I was still full of wondering. Ian managed to get the flu while we were there and I was hoping that he would be back to normal for the big day. On the way to Dalby we needed to call into Toowoomba to meet the marriage celebrant, Mrs Davis. I had to sign some forms and pick up a selection of marriage vows for us to choose from. It was now only a week to the big day, and we had some last minute things to do like choosing our reception menu and speaking to the photographer about what type of photos we wanted taken.

Thank goodness we had arranged one as three days before the wedding, Ian's father who until now I hadn't met, ended up in hospital after a minor stroke and for a time he lost his memory. Ian's mother rang up to tell him and despite being told by his mother it wasn't necessary to drive up to Bundaberg to see his Father, I convinced him that it was his right and he had better go just in case something happened and he would regret it for the rest of his life. Ian and his older brother who was to be our best man went up to see their father and fortunately he did get well enough to attend the wedding. The night before, I met his maternal Grandmother and his younger brother with his wife at the motel. Most of the time I spent looking at them all, trying to work out what sort of people they were and I felt isolated. I could not help but notice that the grandmother failed to show any desire to get to know me. She seemed so sure of herself and the first thought that came to me was—hadn't anything happened in her 80 odd years that would make her want to show me a bit of compassion? Surely she would have had some thought in her mind that this would not have been an easy situation for me to be in.

That night I didn't sleep much. At this point it had not hit home that I was really getting married that day, after all, I had only been back in Australia for 10 days and so much had happened in such a short time. My sister-in-law, my niece and I made it to the hairdresser and were there for nearly two hours. While we were there, guess who walked in? It was Ian's parents who had arrived for the wedding. At this point I had no idea of what they even looked like, so seeing these strangers looking at me for the first time was very emotionally draining. Ian's mother took me by the hand out to the car where she showed me our wedding cake. It was beautifully decorated with emerald green ribbon threaded through it and completed with very fine lace work, and finished off with apricot flowers. At this moment it really hit me that I would be married in just a few hours time.

We only just made it back from the hairdressers in time for the photographer who arrived, taking what turned out to be (regardless of the fact my hair was falling down, as usual), great photographs right through until the reception was over.

Blushing Bride

The Bride and Groom

Our day, 16th July 1994, went off really well. Our chosen colour scheme was off white wedding gown embossed with roses and matching lace with sequins on the bodice and upper arms. The matron of honour's dress was an emerald green suit which she could wear again and we carried apricot floral arrangements which I had brought back from Canada with me, as well as the rings and my wedding gown.

Ian and his brother wore black suits with emerald green bow ties and small matching apricot floral arrangements in their suit lapels. The ceremony was conducted by the celebrant, Mrs Davies, who was very nice and it turned out to be a lovely relaxed ceremony which went off really well. It was in one of the main parks in Dalby and I thought our very late reception was worth having after such a long wait, we didn't get out of the photographers until after 1pm.

Ian was full of surprises, and hadn't given me any clues as to where we were going for our honeymoon, we ended up on Fraser Island off Queensland, staying at the Kingfisher Bay Resort.

At this point I was high as a kite emotionally. I could not believe my luck that someone actually wanted to love me for who I was and wanted to spend the rest of their life with me.

If only I had known what was around the corner, I most likely would not have married anyone at all. When we ended up doing what comes naturally to honeymooners, all I can say is that it was like a bomb had gone off in the memory part of my brain. The best way I can explain it is that the room we were in was only slightly lit and I could just see the outline of what was Ian's face, but suddenly out of the blue, what I was seeing wasn't him and I ended up screaming and desperately pushing him away with all of this strength that seemed to come out of nowhere. It was as if I had been in this situation before, yet I had never voluntarily been in a sexual relationship and suddenly I felt I had to escape in a dreadful hurry. I felt totally panic stricken and when I realised where I had seen this face before, it made things even worse. It was the face I remember when my foster father would hold me down on the bed in the night. I ended up screaming for Ian to stop as I couldn't cope with what was happening. I then had to, in between sobs and tears, try to explain to Ian why I was in such a state, and tell him that it wasn't his fault and he'd done nothing wrong.

From that night on, sexual activity can only be described as a nightmare for me, I felt as if every time Ian touched me I had to get away and I would have a heart attack if I couldn't escape if I needed to. It was a terrible predicament to be in, when I wanted to be with Ian and do what comes naturally with a partner I loved, but at the same time I was scared out of my wits, through no fault of mine or his. It was dreadful to feel that I had to escape and if I didn't feel I could, my heart would pound and I would get all sweaty. I now understood why I had such a dislike for certain people all this time, even though I had been very fortunate to be placed in a secure and loving environment with my foster-mum at the age of 6 years, the damage had already been done, and it left me with serious problems that I wouldn't wish on anyone else. Just imagine trying to get a balance between normal sexual activity and the following problems:

- Can't stand being touched with finger tips or light friction below waist level
- Can't bear to have my arms being pinned down below shoulder level
- Must be able to move my arms at all times
- Can't handle a full body hug if my arms are not free to move
- Do not handle kissing well, either when not having or having sex
- Total panic when my husband puts any body weight on me and just forget the whole idea of touching his genitals.

As you can imagine, these problems cause a lot more problems when your partner chooses not to—or cannot—understand my situation. HELP!!

It is so cruel to be left with these physical issues as it doesn't do anything for the emotional aspect of the relationship either. It's certainly horrific when your brain starts screaming inside your head because you can't handle what's happening on the outside.

I cannot handle hearing children scream or seeing them being roughly handled and I dislike being around people who drank alcohol. It makes me wonder what I had locked away in my memory during the first 6 years of my life, because I definitely knew that this was not a normal reaction if one was being sexually active by choice.

During the days, Ian and I had a blast. You should have seen the bathroom when we tried out the spa, Ian accidentally put a whole bottle of concentrate bubble bath in and the bubbles ended up 12 or more inches above the top of the tub to the point that I couldn't even see his head. Meanwhile the bubbles are moving ever closer to the edge of the carpet. Ian thought that the people outside must have been wondering what on earth was going on as I was laughing so much that my ribs were hurting. For the rest of our time on the island we did the tourist things which included overdosing on chocolate mousse, we had never felt so ill!!

We finally settled into our first little rental home by the Memorial Gardens which was very good as it was so central and I walked most places. There was now one major wardrobe crisis because in the November I still hadn't received my boxes from Canada which I had shipped home in the April, and I was living out of a suitcase. As you can imagine, the novelty had worn off because we had very little linen and our Canadian wedding presents were also in the boxes. I decided I should ring the shipping company to check if the ship had sunk because I hadn't heard anything. I finally found out that my boxes had been sitting at Botany Bay for some time and had come home to Australia via Hong Kong!

I must have been living in a dream world in one sense, because I was as happy as I can ever remember being, but I had no idea of what would soon eventuate.

Every month I wrongly made the assumption that at any minute I would get pregnant as Ian and I had discussed it and it was one of the reasons for me accepting his marriage proposal. We both wanted children. I knew enough about myself to know that I could never have married a person who did not want children. I had decided when I reached 15 years of age that in return for what I had been through, I wanted to be able to hold my own newborn baby in my arms just one time. I wanted to be able to give it the most important things that I never had from my biological mother. As much as this might sound really stupid to anyone reading this, for some reason I used the ability to have my own children as a sense of security because I felt that it could not be taken away from me like other things had been.

In August of 1995, Ian and I found out that we would never be able to conceive. We had been married for nine months and I started to get the feeling that something was very wrong because we had done nothing to prevent a pregnancy from occurring. As I was already 34 years old, I knew that I didn't have a lot of years to spare and just because you get pregnant doesn't guarantee a baby at the end. Ian didn't want to go to the doctor with me. He was so sure I was just worrying too much and why would it be him? Typical male! Finally I just about had enough to the point I was getting very emotional. My monthly cycles were now 45 days in length and I knew that this was not normal for me. We finally went to the doctor with Ian's sample because they usually check the male first; it's the cheaper of the tests. There was a student doctor sitting in as he was doing a bit of learning by watching the different patients' reactions etc.

It was not that easy to ask all of the questions that I would have like to when there is a stranger in the room, even though I realise that they have to learn somewhere, why did it have to by while I was the patient? We were to go back one week later when the results of the tests would be known and for some reason I wasn't too worried, at least we had the ball rolling. Thursday came and off we went again to find out what was going on. Well guess what—the student doctor was still there and then came the awful truth. Ian would never be able to father a child as he didn't have any sperm. I just sat there in silence because it was the last thing that I had thought of. The doctor checked out Ian and did some blood tests which really didn't give us much information about the reason for his zero sperm count.

Before going to find out what the problem was, I thought that maybe it was me that was the cause of the lack of babies, and I was really hoping it was me because I know there's a lot of help available to potential mums with reproductive problems. Also, I am the type of person that I would rather have a problem than see my husband have to face up to something so devastating. I feel sorry for anyone who has to face experiences like this as it was very emotionally draining. We walked home from the doctor in silence as we had not been prepared for what we had just been told; it was like a part of me had just died and I felt numb. It was like my world had come to a complete standstill and I was not aware of time.

Ian rang his parents to tell them and to my horror they didn't even bother to say hello to me, let alone offer any support. Five minutes after he had spoken to his mum, his sister rang to see if we were alright, and I was thankful for that.

Over the next few days it struck me cold, why on earth did the doctor allow the student doctor to remain in the room when he knew exactly what he had to tell us? Why didn't we have any privacy as after all, the doctor knew that it would be devastating news for us? He wasn't to know how we would react. I feel that the doctor, as nice as he was, still had a lot to learn about how to treat your patients with respect and remember how you would like to be treated yourself.

He did refer us to a Repromed Reproductive Unit to find out about donor insemination. We knew now that it would be our only chance of having any children. We were not eligible for adoption because of the short duration of our marriage and my age. While I had been trying to get Ian to the doctor, I had been told by some that I was trying too hard and that I should just forget about it and that it would happen. Well, it's not that easy because how can you forget about it when you get a reminder every month to tell you that you have failed once again. Life is not just like a book that you can just turn the page and it's gone out of sight, out of mind and you just can't turn off and on the desire to have a child of your own just to suite others around you who have no idea what they are saying.

As the weeks went by we told a few of our close friends and when I told one of them on the phone, I felt really sorry for her. She simply said "oh no" and then went deadly quiet. She knew I had been hoping that it was me with the problem and not Ian. Another friend who had been telling me that it was just because I was thinking about it too much, ended up giving me a big hug, which was really quite a surprise.

It's very hard to explain in words what this news did to me emotionally. Here I am thinking one minute that we would have a child who would resemble either one of us or be a total mixture, as far as I was concerned our children would have looked quite cute. Ian is very good looking and I have fine features and limbs and I was a sweet little thing according to photos taken of me at 6 years of age. Now I had to face up to the fact that Ian can never be a biological father. I thought that I was alright for the first 6 weeks or so, I didn't cry and that in its self surprised me. We told my Mum who at that stage was quite sympathetic until we told her of our plan regarding the donor insemination program. I had done a lot of thinking by now and as much as I would have given anything to be able to have Ian's children, I had come to the conclusion that the sperm donor would give us the greatest gift of all—a child, so I didn't have a problem with what we were going to do. We were visiting mum for lunch one Friday and without warning, she just announced to us that God had made it very, very clear to her that we must not go ahead with our plan. She couldn't really give us a reason and as a result I was in total shock why she would not support us in our bid to have at least one child. What really made me angry is that she took Ian aside and showed him some reference in the bible regarding people who did not have children but I have no idea of what she actually said to him as she spoke very softly so I couldn't hear what was being said. From that day I have never spoken to her regarding our attempts to have a baby. I felt it would only put me under more stress than I needed. A person can only handle so much before they crack. It was totally beyond me why on earth she would want me to be denied my one wish in life, a wish I made when I was only 15 years old.

One Monday I got up and I just knew that I was in for a really bad day. Ian through his lack of wisdom just said to me that it didn't matter if we didn't have any children. Well, that was it for me; I just couldn't take it any more as I was totally frustrated. I ended up yelling at him, telling him why I was upset and how I felt just like a piece of junk. His parents had never bothered to speak to me and I had only heard negative comments like "you're not meant to have children" or "you'll have them God's time". The people who think like this always have children of their own, so how on earth would they know what I was feeling inside. I was so upset that by the time Ian decided to give me a hug, it was too late and I just pushed him away and sat in the corner, wanting to be left alone. I never even got a kiss goodbye before he left for work, but then again I was that upset that it probably wouldn't have made a difference anyway.

I knew that I had to talk to somebody as I felt that I was going out of my mind and I didn't know what to do with myself anymore. I had been given a phone number of a support group called Oasis; it's for people with fertility problems. I decided that I didn't have anything to lose, so I rang the number and ended up speaking with this nice person called Tracey for two and a half hours. Ian still can't understand how I could talk to someone I had never met, for that long. As a result of the phone call I did feel much better and I even made a real nice tea for us, but Ian wouldn't even eat it because in his mind, he thought I might have been trying to poison him—he really thought I was going around the twist that morning, and of course, that did nothing for my low self-esteem. Eventually I started to feel much better and began to take an interest in life again.

We first went to the Repromed Reproductive Unit in September 1995 after seeing a specialist who just happened to be the same one who had fixed up my fallopian tubes 5 years earlier. We both had to have quite a few blood tests just to make sure we didn't have any diseases which might affect the outcome of our attempts. I didn't like having to have them, as after all, I knew I didn't have the diseases they were testing for and hey! Don't I have any privacy anymore? Also people who get pregnant without any help don't have to have them. We also had to see their counsellor which was just a waste of her time as well as ours, because we knew what we were trying to do, so why did we need to waste our time and money? Finally the consent form was signed in the October, so now I could have a go. It was too late to start in the November as the beginning of my next cycle had already been and gone, so I would have to wait until next month.

Now it was my turn at last. I was getting a real chance and for once I was very happy to get my period. Off I went to Adelaide to stay at one of my friend's homes for a couple of days. Every morning I would get up at 6am to get to the clinic on time as we had to be there before 8am to have a blood test done. The blood test was so they could see what my hormones were doing and tell whether or not the levels were right for the insemination. It was done over two days to give it the best chance of hitting the jackpot. Now we just had to wait and see. I would know in about two weeks either by blood test, or when my next cycle started.

I had only been home a couple of days and Ian asked me "how is he this morning?". First of all I wasn't sure what he was talking about—and then it clicked, he was talking about the baby which might just be in there, so I had to explain that it might not have worked as it was only my first try and I didn't want to get too hopeful, only to come down with a big crash. I was right, it hadn't worked, but hey! I did get my first chance, so I was still pretty happy.

I was hoping to go again in January, but Ian soon crushed that plan by saying that we couldn't afford it. Once again I was totally devastated to the point that I felt like running away, not because I didn't love him anymore, but for two reasons. Firstly, I could not cope with the fact that this man who cannot father a child was telling me that if I went to Adelaide for another chance to try and fall pregnant, not to bother coming home and secondly, I was scared stiff that I might just have an early menopause and miss out altogether. I tried to explain that you can't just sign a consent form and then say I'm not going to go. I was definitely at an emotional low now and for quite a few days I felt very alone.

I finally got another chance in February 1996, only to find out that I had not released an egg that month, after having an injection to make any egg come down if it was going to. Before I went home after spending 10 days in Adelaide just waiting, I had to see the doctor and I was told that the staff at the clinic were getting confused. I was given a prescription for some tablets that came with a $50. 00 price tag. These pills were supposed to make you more fertile and thus increase your chance of falling pregnant.

Late March early April would be my next chance as we were going away for 12 days to Kangaroo Island for my school reunion, and I would not be home at the right time in May. When I called at the beginning of my cycle I was instructed to start taking the pills, so I thought to myself, this is great—I might just be lucky enough to find out that I'm pregnant for my birthday which was on April 28.

My birthday was going quite nicely until we heard on the radio just after lunch that 35 innocent people had been shot at Port Arthur in Tasmania.

I couldn't believe my ears. Here I was celebrating my 35th birthday, 35 years of life and for each of those years, some poor soul had died. For the remainder of the day I was feeling horrible thinking of all the families who had been affected by that murdering moron.

I needed to visit the doctor to find out more information regarding the tablets because nobody at the fertility unit had bothered to tell me anything about them. I was starting to feel that they were overlooking the need for communication between the patient and the staff. I was told to go down on day 13 of my cycle, so off I went quite happily at 4. 30am on Sunday morning with my two blood samples, taken over the last two days. After a good trip down I was there on time so then I just had to wait until 1. 30pm to find out when I had to go back. I had gone out for lunch at a friend's place and was having a really good time until I rang to get the results. The news was that I had already ovulated, and it was too late. I couldn't believe what I had just been told and my world went into slow motion. Rosie, the nurse, in her effort to be nice, simply said "I guess you're disappointed", I just said yes, and hung up. I was far from happy because I had made the effort to get there, only to be told it was too late. I just didn't know what to think as I was doing what they asked and this was what I got in return. The two blood samples that were taken over the two days were not even used, and that ticked me off because I had to have them done by the doctor on duty at the hospital both times, and it took at least twenty minutes as my veins are not as good as they used to be, a result of constant puncturing. I went home on the Monday and by Tuesday I was so upset and frustrated, I got in the car and just drove, not caring whether I lived or died.

I found out later that the doctors knew that the tablets could work from day 10 on, and as far as I'm concerned, that's when I should have been told to be in Adelaide, not three days later as instructed. I went to see one of the local doctors to find out if there was anything I could do to make sure that this sort of stupid mistake didn't occur again, and his advice was just go earlier if I felt I needed to.

Emotionally, I was a total wreck I just wished I was dead because I felt like I was falling down a dark hole and I didn't know when I would hit bottom. I had also come to the place of feeling that I couldn't take anymore of this type of emotional pain. There is nothing worse than feeling as if you're just a number, and decisions regarding your course of treatment are usually made by someone you never get to meet.

I have to be quite honest, I did take a while to get to the point of being able to handle the clinic's mistake. If they had told me what could happen, I would have been expecting it and not reacted the way I did. I still had really bad days where I just had to lay down and hope that I would feel better when I woke up. It's very hard to cope when your emotional pain hurts so much that you don't know what to do with yourself. Ian interpreted this as me being lazy, but what else was I supposed to do—have a nervous breakdown?

When we went to Kangaroo Island for our holiday, I was really enjoying myself until one day we were driving along and Ian just blurted out that I would not be going to the clinic anymore after we got home. I went into shock and thought to myself, how could he say that when he knew that I had been telling my friends that I was going to have another try when we got back? His reason again was that we couldn't afford it, but I knew he was lying because I had worked out our finances. I told him I could move to the Flinders Medical Centre where the same treatment only cost $45 (out of pocket), instead of $200 at the clinic I was going to. Well, again he had another excuse, he didn't want to have to go to Adelaide to see more people and sign more forms. I suggested that I stay home that month and try again in June, but that he wouldn't stop me from going. I pointed out to him that he'd better make up his mind whether or not he really wanted a child because he had no idea what he was doing to me emotionally. I almost died when he mentioned the word adultery, as this was another of his excuses for me not going to the clinic, so I had to do some very fast talking to save myself because I knew if he won that time, it would be the end for me. I rang one of my friends who had to adopt her children, for some urgent advice and after I told her what was going on she just said "Debbie, you've come too far to stop now." That stayed with me and it gave me a lot of encouragement to keep going. I honestly believed that when I presented Ian with a newborn baby to hold in his arms, he would understand why I had been so persistent for so long. I knew he loved kids and he had told people that he would love to have some, and every time he saw a baby his face would light up.

In June I made a visit to the local doctor regarding a mark on my face which was really an excuse to see him about Ian because I could no longer handle how he was treating me. I had had just about enough and I felt that I couldn't take anymore. When I told the doctor that I nearly ran the car into a stobie pole, he realised how bad I felt and told me to call him if I was feeling bad. He also asked to see Ian. I didn't feel like I was worth much anymore and I honestly didn't know just how many times I could take being stabbed in the heart. In June the tablets didn't work the way they were meant to, there were two good sized follicles but the hormone levels didn't rise to allow the eggs to be released and so the cycle was cancelled. Then I had to go to see my clinic doctor who put me on daily injections of Humogen (H. M. G.) for my next try and if that didn't work, he wanted us to go on the G. I. F. T. program. I happened to mention that I didn't like injections (nothing like being honest with your doctor!). He just looked up at me and said "it depends on how much you want a baby". I thought to myself, boy oh boy, your communications skills could do with a bit of a brush up!

He then quickly rushed over the G. I. F. T. program and but because I had already read about it at least ten times, I wasn't really interested. I knew Ian would probably say NO as we are not on a big income and the out of pocket expenses are $700 per try, so I just hoped the injections would work.

In July I attended an Oasis support meeting on the subject of male infertility. I was hoping I would find some enlightening information. It was a very interesting meeting and I found out that all of the tests that could have been done for Ian were not done, so I started thinking what ARE they doing to us? The day before I left to go to Adelaide for the meeting, Ian told me that God had made him like he was for a reason, and he also proceeded to tell me that God had also made me defective and that was why my mother gave me to the welfare, and that I was not meant to have children. This was the icing on the cake as I never in all my life expected to have my differences with my mother thrown in my face by my husband. I decided that I would give him the scare of his life and not return home when I said I would, just to see if I was worth anything to him. It worked and he reported me missing to the police!

I had another go in July with the injections and I was starting to get used to them, so I was given them for another 9 days and then on the Monday night I was given an HAG injection to make the egg release on Wednesday morning. The insemination was done twice, Tuesday and then again on Wednesday morning, this time with the I. U. I. method to give me a better chance of conceiving. Now I just had to wait the two weeks for the outcome. During this time I knew Ian had been going to see the doctor for his man to man talks but I just played dumb and waited to see what happened. As it turned out, the poor doctor forgot why Ian was there, probably due to the fact that had just had three weeks off. I'm not exactly sure what Ian got out of the visits because of his attitude, but I did notice that he was more talkative about his feelings. Ian did however have three comments about me after seeing the doctor, "I have a problem", "I want a child too badly" and that I "shouldn't bother the doctor". The doctor gave him a pamphlet regarding counselling, so I took it as a hint that the doctor felt Ian needed to get some help from somewhere and so I said we have to sort out this situation and I made an appointment for us both on 16 September. I was hoping that something positive would come out of it so I would have some idea of what direction I was going.

Our consent form was to run out in October so I had just a month to go before I had no more opportunities without Ian's written consent. I have to be honest, I didn't know how I would handle it then as I had no idea what direction Ian would take. On his birthday I decided that I had to see a Counsellor myself as I could no longer handle all the negative comments.

Wendy (my counsellor) was very nice and her advice to me was to try and ignore where the comments were coming from and that I needed to work out a "plan B" for myself, just in case Ian didn't change his current position. I decided that I would have a good talk to his mother to try and find out why he seemed to take twice as long to comprehend things. Well, it seems that he had been like it since he was young, but the good news was that he does catch up, so that gave me a bit of hope. I also found out that his family had the impression that I was also infertile. No wonder I was getting negative remarks, I had no idea of what Ian had been or not been telling them. His mother went quiet once she realised that she didn't know the whole story and I also told her that I nearly tried to commit suicide because I felt that I couldn't take any more stabs in the heart about this whole situation. I was just hoping that she would make an effort to be more supportive towards us on an emotional level if at all possible, as we needed all the support we could get. I then had a talk to my Mum and kindly told her to say nothing regarding our fertility situation as we were the ones that would or would not have a family and therefore we needed to do what we thought was best for us.

In September I went to see the local doctor regarding my own fertility as I was not totally convinced that I needed all the drugs that were being used on me. I had never been given a chance to really prove beyond doubt that I needed the H. M. G. injections because the tablets I was taking were available in 100mg as well as 50mg. I was never even given a try on the higher dose. I honestly got the feeling that they were pushing me up to the top of the technology ladder far too quickly because they never asked for my input on how I was feeling about things and hey— nothing like getting money out of desperate people. I was just hoping that the doctor could do something about finding out what was really going on with my own fertility.

My visit was well worth the time as I found out what really happened when Ian visited the doctor. The doctor played dumb just to see where Ian was coming from regarding the whole situation. The doctor concluded that Ian was only hearing what he wanted to. At least now I knew that I am not totally stupid and that other people could also see what Ian was like. We had our appointment with the counsellor on Monday night and I wondered what the result would be. I also had an appointment to see a visiting Gynaecologist on the 20th of September to see if he could work on my level of fertility so at least then I would know exactly where I stood and hopefully he could work out exactly how much assistance I really needed. I really wanted to be given a decent chance of becoming pregnant, without the G. I. F. T. program.

The specialist was as described by our local doctor, a decent man, even though he told me that people using donated gametes don't have any say. He said he would ring up the Flinders Medical Centre to see what they had to offer me. I knew for sure that if the doctors there couldn't help me, that I would have no children. Ian made it very clear that he would not give consent for the G. I. F. T. program, even if we had the money, because he was against the use of drugs. I might have innocently created this problem myself because when we first went to see the doctor at the clinic, he mentioned that he thought that my best chance of getting pregnant would be if I went on the G. I. F. T. program or tried I.V. F.

I. V. F. At that time I knew that Ian would not allow it due to the out of pocket expenses which were about $700 per try. I also knew that it was common knowledge that a lot of women go on the I. V. F and G. I. F. T. programs when it's not really needed, but doctors put them on it because of the big money involved. Ian didn't want to understand the H. M. G. and H. C. G. injections were not totally drugs as they were both taken from a woman's urine. I began to wonder why he was being so pig headed as after all, I was trying to give him the ultimate gift, a child that he would normally not have. Maybe I was stupid or something, but I thought that he would think I was special and hey, what about my only wish for my whole lifetime? Doesn't that count for something?

We did get to see Wendy regarding our situation, even though Ian didn't want to go—he didn't see that we had a problem. Wendy told him all of the things in less than an hour that I had been trying to tell him for the previous six months. I was just hoping that some of it would sink in because he couldn't stagnate indefinitely, there comes a time when you have to move on.

Even though I knew that it would hurt a lot on an emotional level, I decided that I would have to give up my chances at Wakefield Street in an effort to be fair to Ian, because I did realise that $200 is a lot of money when we only got $11.00 an hour. The consent form expired in October so I was just hoping that Ian didn't take it for granted that I would give up opportunities which couldn't be regained in the future.

On the October long weekend, I had to have a blood sample taken (ordered by the new specialist), to check if I was releasing an egg by myself. It had to be done by our family doctor as the sister on duty couldn't get my veins to come up, nothing like being different! I have to be quite honest; I was a bit worried about the results for a couple of reasons. Firstly Ian had said that he didn't want me to use drugs and secondly he didn't think that it was worth trying if my overall chances were less than 50%. I didn't feel that this was really fair, if I was in his shoes I wouldn't have been dictating the conditions in which a child, which is nothing less than a gift, was conceived. Ian had not provided another sample yet to really prove beyond doubt the he could not father his own children, so I said he would have to go with the flow or we would be left behind. I had been in contact with a couple of families who had donor insemination children and they both said the same thing—that it was well worth it because they couldn't imagine life without children.

I went to get the blood test results on the Thursday after the long weekend, only to find out that the blood sample hadn't been sent away to be tested, I guess it was still sitting in the fridge over at the hospital, so I got no results. Friday was a bad day for me as I cried most of the day feeling physically and emotionally drained. I hadn't slept the night before and now I would have to wait until the following week until the results were available. Ian wasn't very understanding, he just said the doctor couldn't charge me as he had done nothing. I wasn't very happy with his attitude because once again he was using money to measure everything. I explained that the doctor still had to write a letter for us to take to the Flinders Medical Centre so we could start the whole process AGAIN!

I sometime felt that I had had enough, I wondered how much more I could go through without Ian's support. It wasn't nice to have even more strangers looking at me and heaps more blood tests, when I had already lost count of the number of times I had done it all in the previous year. The day before we went for our first appointment at the Flinders Medical Centre, I finally got the results of the blood tests. Hooray, I had released an egg by myself so I couldn't be classed as infertile. Now it just left me with the question of why had the doctors at Wakefield Street so eager to use drugs when they didn't even bother to prove I really needed them.

Well, that just about sums up the first phase of my experience in the world of infertility. I was only hoping that the next phase would be more rewarding and not so emotionally draining and painful.

On our first appointment at the Flinders Medical Centre, we met a new doctor at the fertility clinic and he seemed to be quite nice and at least he explained the results of Ian's tests to us so we now had a much better understanding of why things were the way they were. We found out that I had only four more attempts available before I was out, because of a lack of donors. Ian was a lot happier at this clinic so that was one thing to be grateful for. I have to admit that I could have choked the doctor when he asked Ian if he had fathered children with anyone else, I thought to myself why would we be there if that was the case? All of the routine blood tests were repeated and I far as I was concerned, that was just Government waste because Ian and I hadn't changed our sexual behaviour, so there was no chance that we could have acquired any diseases. But, we had to go along with them and hope they didn't take five months to tell us the results.

Our next appointment was on 19th November. We had to see the nursing staff who were to explain everything to us about the unit. We also had to see their counsellor, Karen, which I didn't mind at all, it would be a good opportunity to tell her what we had already been through.

We intended to leave home at 6am and pick up our friend on the way as she wanted a lift to Adelaide to visit her new granddaughter. We only just made it out of town and the car broke down, so we had to crawl back home and borrow our friend's car. We had plenty of time for our appointment and after seeing mum for a few minutes on the way, we arrived for our first appointment with the nursing sister at 11am, only to be told that our 1pm appointment had been changed to 2pm. We had to explain that this was too late as Ian had to be back for work at 6pm. I also had to work so I was happy when they said we could see the counsellor straight away and then we would be finished by 2pm.

At the counsellor appointment, I told Karen a bit about what Ian had been like and a couple of times it must have been obvious that she didn't like what he was saying to me as her face went dead straight. Apart from that, the interview went really well and she asked us to come back when it suited us, or that I could go back by myself if I wanted to, next time I was down. Karen explained to Ian that if I didn't cry when I needed to that I would end up having a nervous breakdown and it would cost him a lot more than a phone call to Adelaide. She also made it very clear that I had lost something, and that it was not all made up in my mind. I was really pleased that we had seen her as I felt that I had been reacting normally to the situation, and I wasn't weird as Ian had suggested. As much as I felt angry and frustrated with Ian, sometimes I also felt sorry for him as it became clear to me that his parents made no effort to offer him any emotional support during that whole 15 months. I don't know why I wasted my time talking to his mother earlier that year, asking for her support, but she didn't seem to hear what I had been saying. I now realised that all Ian and I had was each other and his parents didn't care enough to take time to see what we were going through regarding our fertility situation. I decided that if I ever got pregnant, I was going to make them feel left out so then they would know how I had felt for the past 15 months.

Mum has come around a bit so to speak, at least she's now talking to me about it a little. Needless to say she doesn't forget the God factor, so I just have to close my ears. As for Ian's parents, I feel that they have a lot to learn in regards to communication. I had reached the stage of feeling that if they couldn't be bothered talking to me when I'm meant to be their daughter-in-law, that I couldn't be bothered making any effort to involve them in my life, they were much like strangers to me. Ian and I had been married for over two years now and not once had his parents every acknowledged my birthday by card or phone. It only cost 45 cents for a stamp plus the card, and a phone call doesn't need to be more than two minutes duration if you don't have a lot of money, but Ian's parents couldn't use that as an excuse. Like I might have mentioned before, people that have never been through any hard experiences can be very shallow and only think about themselves.

I was meant to be back at the clinic in February but I wasn't sure as I hadn't had a period since 15 October and now it was 27 November. The last score on my hormone blood test was disgusting as out of a score of 30 to 35, I only got up to 3. No wonder I hadn't had a period.

Thursday the 12 December was a really bad day for me as I just felt like crying all day. I now felt that I had nearly had enough and I wasn't making any progress and felt violated by the new clinic. I couldn't see why I had to keep giving blood samples all the time when I knew that I didn't have any of the diseases they were testing for. It only added to the trauma of the whole experience as far as I'm concerned. Not only that, but as nice as the nurse was to us, surely she didn't have to tell me when to go to my local doctor to get a pap smear done. I think it stinks because if I wasn't married nobody would bother to tell me that I needed one. I waited until I was 33 before I married and not once was I asked by any doctor if ever I'd had one done before. I had gotten to the point of being sick and tired of being poked at, and spreading my legs for everybody so I decided that I would ask the doctor if I could just skip it as I didn't need anymore intrusion than necessary at the moment.

I was hoping that we could claim money from the Pats Scheme, which is for patients who have to travel 200 kilometres for treatment. To make things worse, the next day we received a Christmas card from Ian's sister in law and on one side it had a nice Christmas message and on the other side she had written "sorry to hear you are not pregnant yet, but God may have bigger things planned for you both." Of course, to my horror, Ian agreed with her so I just said to him, "what are the plans and how long do we have to wait?"

I don't understand why people who haven't had any difficulty getting their children feel that they have the right to say things like that, and besides, who the hell would write this in a Christmas card to start with? It is totally beyond me how people can be so cruel in their comments. They made me feel very drained and I was fast coming to the conclusion that I was rowing a canoe upstream against everybody else. On 17 December I decided that if my hormones didn't greatly improve, I might have to pull out because I didn't know how much more I could take emotionally, maybe it would just be better that I quit while I still had a few attempts up my sleeve, just in case I felt like going back later, instead of using up all of my attempts and coming out with nothing. So, I was damned if I didn't and damned if I did.

It was now 18 December 1996, and also day 21, off to the clinic for another dreaded needle, and guess what? This time it all had to be done by another doctor, so now it's four down and one to go. I hoped the results would be much better than last time as I had been trying to eat as much fish as possible. Hooray, hooray, this month's test result was 37. I could hardly believe my ears when Meredith the nurse told me that it was nothing short of a major accomplishment. Meredith told me to phone on 31 January, and to tell them about my cycles so they would know when I needed to come down.

To be honest, I didn't totally enjoy the festive season that year as I feel that Christmas is mainly geared up for kids and as we don't have any, I felt that I had a big void in my life. 28th December was a really bad day for me. I felt totally drained and tired to the point of just wanting to lay down for most of the afternoon, sleeping and having the shakes at the same time. I had never been like this before and hoped I never would be again. It felt like I would have to get help from somewhere because a person could not function like this for very long.

On 2 January 1997, I went against my wishes to have the Pap test because as the doctor said "we just have to keep them (the fertility clinic) happy". I thought to myself, what about me? I had told the doctor it was a waste of his time. They could have done the test at the clinic if they wanted to. I now felt totally violated and I just wanted to be left alone, I really felt that I had nearly had enough. The examination did not do much for me, I hated it, and probably due to the sexual abuse I had endured as a child. I told the doctor that I wouldn't be having the test done anymore. I did ask him how long I could stay away from doctors if and when I ever got pregnant. I really felt that I needed a mental break, a person can only handle so much and I was pleased with his answer when he said I wouldn't need to go until I was at least 12 weeks along. I'm happy with that, after all, nothing can be done to stop a miscarriage if it's going to happen.

1997

In January, I rang up to get my results from the last day 21 test. This time the specialist told me that he couldn't work out the result because even though the blood was taken on the fifth day, my cycle was 22 days long so they weren't exactly sure if I had released an egg, but the second time I spoke to him, he said that it as most likely that I had. He also told me that it just might have been too close for comfort for me to have any chance in February. I couldn't believe my ears. I thought to myself, I don't believe this is happening again. Maybe I was wrong, but I thought that when you were told by somebody that they would do something in February, they would stick to their word. At the last Clinic if that had been said to me, it meant I was going to have either a natural cycle or a cycle with drugs. This doctor said that it was possible that they might decide to let me miss a cycle so that could control the next one with drugs, I mentioned to him that nobody told me I needed to take any. I had to ring up on 'Tuesday morning to see what was going on. Now I was beginning to feel as if I had jumped from the frying pan into the fire. I didn't have the basic right as a human being to say what happened to my own body anymore. I had some really bad days as a result of this, and I was dreading what was going to be said on Tuesday. I had an awful feeling that I wouldn't be going to have a go this month as I was meant to. I hadn't told Ian what was going on yet, I really didn't know how to tell him as I found out that he was hoping I would get pregnant soon.

Well, I rang up on the Tuesday and as I had thought, I couldn't have a go that month, instead I had to send the useless temperature charts down so they could work out what they thought they should do with me.

I could not believe just how stupid they were being as since November I had been having monthly blood tests done to help them work out what to do with me when I start at their clinic. I really didn't know why they were messing around with me as they had a copy of my file from the last clinic and surely that would tell them a lot. I just cried my eyes out as I couldn't understand just how they thought that they could play with my emotions the way they are. Don't they realise that we people with major fertility problems have enough to cope with. I had built up my hopes that maybe, just maybe I might just be lucky this time, as after all it had been six months since I had my last try.

I was told to ring in on Monday the 3rd of February to find out what was going on, and then told to ring on Wednesday, this time the excuse was that the doctor didn't come into the clinic till Wednesday, so why on earth was I told to phone on Monday to start with?

Well, guess what? I got a call at about 2pm on Wednesday from the clinic and I had just been thinking to myself that at least I would know what to do well before the beginning of my next cycle, thinking to myself that I would have been given the instructions over the phone regarding the dosage for the Clomid etc, because I had explained to Meredith that I already had a prescription for the tablets and that I would only need to get the instructions about the dosage. I'd been told I would be able to have a go in March. How wrong could I have been? I was told that I would have to see the doctor on the 5th of March to talk about the Clomid tablets. It was totally beyond me how and why I needed to talk to a doctor for 30 minutes about Clomid tablets when I had taken them before. I just said to Meredith what about my go that I was meant to have that month as I had already worked out in my mind that it would probably be too late to try that month as I had to start taking the pills on the 5th day of my cycle. Her excuse was that they didn't know when my next cycle would start. Maybe I was too sensitive, I had been brought up to believe that you kept your word because you could never know how it could affect someone if you didn't

I was getting sick and tired of feeling my heart just sink after I had been told that I couldn't go to the clinic because of some weak excuse. I had thought Ian was bad, but these people should have known better. I know we were only in the public hospital system, but enough is enough for anybody with infertility problems. As far as I could see I should have been given a choice of having a go or not in February without drugs, after all—it's my body isn't it and Ian and I are the ones who have to put up with the outcome. I was really feeling that I didn't have any control over what was happening to my own body anymore. I got the feeling that they just thought I was an emotionless puppet with strings that anyone could pull whenever they felt like it.

On Friday 7th February, I spoke to Karen the counsellor, because I was now at a point of not knowing how much longer I could put up with what was going on. I told her what had been happening and how I had no idea why they were messing me around the way they were, and she tried to get me an earlier appointment, but to no avail. She also tried to find out what was going on and again it seemed that I had not been told everything, Karen was told that the doctor might want to do a scan just to check out my ovaries before I could start on Clomid again. One thing we did manage to find out was I could get the generic band of Clomid which was a difference of $30 per try, so that was one good thing in our favour. I asked Meredith why on earth the scan, if it was so important, couldn't be done before 5th March by a nurse and the then doctor could work out the dose and just tell me over the phone. It seemed that in an effort to cut costs at the hospital they hadn't trained any nurses to do scans which in itself didn't make any sense to me. I was really ticked off because I had told them I had my scan pictures from the other hospital and they were only six months old and that I could post them down, but I was told that they weren't going to be good enough. It was about this time that I decided not to do the stupid temperature charts because I didn't need the daily reminder that I had something wrong with my own fertility—up till now I had no idea that I was having problems of my own with fertility. I was at the point of nearly having had enough as this whole thing had now been going on for nearly two years. Finally it got to my 5th March appointment and I certainly was not in the best of moods as I knew it was all just a waste of time and effort. When I arrived at the clinic I saw Meredith and she said to me "are you looking for us Debbie?" And my reply was "not really", so I think that she got my point. She wouldn't look me in the face so I had a feeling Karen must have said something to her regarding recent events.

I didn't have to wait very long to see the doctor and when I walked in he just said "what's happening?" and I replied "nothing". He went on to say that I hadn't been there since September and I just simply said "I know". I was then given a talk about the risks in connection with Clomid. Needless to say I had already educated myself, and so far this visit was a complete waste of my time. I then had to have a stupid vaginal scan done just to keep the doctor happy as he said that the consultation could not continue without it. Nothing like a bit of blackmail, because at this stage of the visit I hadn't been told what dosage of pills I would need to take. The doctor had to admit that I was right when he saw the screen, as I had already told him—it was a waste of time. I was also told that if I had three or more follicles of the correct size, the insemination would not be done which simply didn't make any sense at all as a person took the pills to become more fertile to start with. I was far from happy as city people didn't seem to think how ridiculous it was to get someone to drive 400 kilometres just for a one minute test.

I finally got to have my first try in April, but I was to scared to be hopeful, just as I was real scared of having the plug pulled on me because of something over which I had no control. I might sound a bit fussy, but after being in a private clinic I found the public system a bit humiliating to say the least as it was run more like a production line and a couple of nurses spoke about me as if I was just a number, not once mentioning my name. On my first day I told one of the nursing staff off because I couldn't see how an adult needed to be told just how to sit on a chair! I think she got the hint as she backed off by saying that I wasn't stupid, I don't think she wanted to make a fool of herself in front of the doctor and the other nurse. I was very relieved when they didn't find more than two follicles. As usual, the nurse who tried to get the blood samples had a bit of trouble but it was nothing new to me so I just had to be patient. Apart from having to put up with three different male doctors (who I had never seen before), doing the scans—which I was far from comfortable with, the first three days went really well. Tuesday was pretty horrible as the first nurse was unsuccessful at getting the blood sample, so she went and got somebody else who would be able to get it. It turned out to be the same nurse I had told off earlier. I told her she would be able to get it out of my wrist, but her excuse was that there were too many nerves there and I thought to myself here we go again! I let her try until she started to twist the needle around like a screwdriver. Suddenly I felt really sick in the stomach and with that I told her that she wasn't having another go which she wanted to, so she said I could have Wednesday off for which I was thankful. I made my way straight to the coffee shop and bought the first piece of cheesecake to get sugar into my blood. One of the staff concluded that that it was hard to get my blood because my blood clots very quickly. My personal thought was that they simply weren't very good at getting blood to start with. I had to have another scan on the Friday just to check if the follicles were still growing. After it was done I then had to have another blood test which wasn't too bad. While all of this was going on I was taken to get a hot drink, so I think that I was the envy of the other patients in the waiting room. Finally I was told what the plan for me was and to my horror it included an injection in the bum to get the egg to release 36 hours later, thus allowing them to do the insemination on Saturday and Sunday mornings. The needle didn't hurt as the nurse put some local anaesthetic with it. At least now I could relax and just hope that something good was going to happen, I did anything to avoid myself thinking about it.

Fortunately I hadn't got my hopes up too much as I didn't get pregnant; a blood test on day 25 showed that I did not release an egg. I was told that I could take 150mg of the generic Clomid a day, for my next try. I was very lucky in the fact that I didn't seem to have any side effects that were mentioned in the information sheet.

It was now June and at last I was having another go. This was only my third try since July 1996. Off I went down on day 12 and lucky for me, I didn't miss as I had with the first dose of tablets. I had a blood test taken on day 10 so they would have something to compare the next one with. It had gone from 1000 to 1400 in two days, so I was really pleased. The scan showed that I had 3 follicles to start with, but one of them just died, leaving me with one of a perfect size and a one slightly smaller. According to Kerrie, this cycle was much better than the first time. The insemination was done on Sunday and Monday morning after I had been given an HMG injection to release the egg. Overall I was really pleased that this time things went much better, so now I had to just wait till the 18th June to find out if I had a chance of getting pregnant. When I rang up to find out what level my hormones had gone to, I was very surprised to find out it was at 59. Well, I was on a high as never before had I gotten a score that high. At least now I knew I had a very good chance of getting pregnant so I just had to wait. As I half expected, I didn't get pregnant and I cried my eyes out. I knew I only had five more chances left before it was over. Ian saw just how upset I was, and to my surprise, admitted that he had not had any goes. I was shocked as this was the first time since this started that he actually admitted his infertility.

In September, I thought I would get another chance but it wasn't to be. Karen, the clinic's counsellor, rang to say that she wanted to see Ian as the clinic had been finding out that some of the families who had donor children, their husbands were leaving the marriages as they never accepted the children as their own. Karen figured that the husbands didn't have the courage to say no to being on the donor program. We made an appointment for early in the month as I wanted to have another go as soon as possible. I rang up to put my name down, only to be told to call the next day as they (the staff) were busy. I thought, fair enough, and the next day I was in Adelaide, so I rang up from a telephone box, only to be told I couldn't come during my next cycle. I simply couldn't believe it as I was real hopeful that this would be my lucky try. The excuse that they gave was that they had been told Ian and I had an appointment with Karen. I asked them to still put my name down and if the session didn't go well, then I could cancel it, as with the insemination there is no fancy technology used. I was told no again and I literally felt all the energy leave my body starting from my head down to my feet. I had to sit in the car for a while as I felt totally numb and betrayed. I never thought Karen would go behind my back and do this to me. It was nearly more than I could handle, especially as Ian had been quite happy for me to go to Adelaide that month and now they had pulled the rug from under my feet, so as a result I felt totally emotionally drained.

When we eventually got the appointment it was pretty draining as Karen had to ask Ian if he wanted to quit the program. There was no point me thinking that there was a chance of me continuing if in fact, he didn't want it. He told her he wanted to continue, but felt that he had no say and no control of the situation. How on earth did he think I felt, as after all, he had been controlling me from when the whole thing started. Karen suggested to Ian that if it would make him feel better, he could write her a small note to say he was happy for me to be in Adelaide, so she gave him some paper for the purpose. When we got back to the carport, I just blew my top as I now felt smaller than an ant. Hey! I was 36 years old and I didn't feel that I should be treated like a young child going on a kindergarten excursion. My self-esteem had already hit rock bottom. Ian did acknowledge that he would love any child which I gave birth to, so that was a great relief in itself.

I managed to have another try at the end of October, but despite having what (the staff and I) thought was a great cycle, I came up with nothing again. The hormones went up really well and I had three large follicles which gave us all the impression that I had a really good chance of it working this time. I was given the egg release injection as usual, after now having to pay $15.00 out of my own pocket which I hadn't had to do before. Over the next three days I had six straws of the donation inseminated and this gave me a lot of hope. I felt I couldn't miss this time. I went home full of hope, thinking wow, at least I had a good chance this time, only to be very disappointed when I got my next period. I simply didn't have the courage to go back for a while; it was beyond me how on earth I could have missed. Ian was also getting a bit ridiculous with his "we can't afford it" rubbish so as usual, I kept my mouth shut. knew if I rocked the boat I would be the one who would be tipped out. I also realised that I couldn't keep carrying all of the emotional strain by myself much longer, so I started talking to a couple of friends who I felt comfortable with and they said the same thing, that Ian had not treated me right. I found that it did ease the pain a bit if I could release it through talking with somebody, I didn't want to get to the same level of despair as I had before.

1998

I didn't know when I would try again, but I knew that I wanted to cut apricots to give myself a bit of extra cash. Ian (for a joke) said just before Christmas that he wanted some children for Christmas and low and behold, Kirsty, our social worker, rang and asked if we would be willing to take in three foster children for about three weeks, and of course Ian said yes. Cassie and her brother Daniel turned up on the Friday night and it didn't take too long to realise that they had a lot of emotional problems. Daniel was the devil in disguise. On the Monday morning Krystal, their younger sister, arrived, and the real fun began. Daniel was only with us for two weeks because we couldn't handle his behaviour. He was becoming physically abusive towards me so I told the welfare that they had to come and get him. After he left, it was like heaven compared to what we had put up with, and by now even Ian realised that we couldn't help him. He had major emotional problems which by no means were his fault. His parents had let him down—nobody else.

Cassie and Krystal remained with us until July 1998 and in that time we saw many improvements which made being a foster parent worthwhile, but it did make one wonder just how many chances parents should be given to pull themselves together, before the plug is pulled on them. Krystal was the type of child I would have loved to adopt, I had to admit I was growing to love her and I knew I would never forget her. As a result of the girls' stay with us, the time passed quite quickly regarding my attempts to get pregnant, for the last two or three months we were expecting they would be moved on to an Aboriginal foster placement because the Aboriginal people don't like their children being cared for by non-Aboriginal people, but if they weren't willing to do it themselves, they shouldn't complain because we didn't deny the girls contact with their own people or culture. In March we went to see the doctor at the clinic to sign the consent forms because Ian had decided I could only go to Adelaide two more times and then it was be over, regardless of the outcome of each trip to the clinic.

I will never forget the day, it was Friday 13th and also the day we had to give poor Roonie away to the dog shelter, because we had done everything to try and stop her from barking so much, but nothing worked. We didn't want to give her up as we had had her for nearly three years and she was part of our family. To me she was very special; she always knew when I was very upset because of our infertility situation. She seemed to have the ability to show me compassion in her own doggy style which made up for Ian's lack of support. It had been very had to cope with that sometimes. One of my worst fears was that if my last two attempts at getting pregnant failed, I honestly didn't know how I would cope on my own without Ian's support as he didn't have any concept of emotional pain.

This was also the day Ian went to Queensland on the plane for five days for a family reunion and to my horror, he told me at the airport that today was his lucky day. Well, I just simply couldn't believe my ears, to me this was one of the worst days of our lives, and I felt totally empty. It was totally horrible as I drove the two and a half hours home by myself in the rain. I might as well have had a sun roof open on the car because I was crying my eyes out all the way home, to the point of almost not being able to see where I was going. I was being tormented by the last look on Roonie's face, an image I wouldn't forget for a long time. When I realised that Ian had made up his mind that he would only allow me to go to the clinic two more times, regardless of the fact that I was entitled to go three more times, I went to see our GP and explained my new tour of hell. He gave me a support letter to be given to the clinic if I needed to. I had been told that if I had too many follicles the insemination wouldn't be done because they didn't want to risk multiple births. Quite ironic when you think about it, as I had been pumped full of fertility drugs that can help you have more than one child at a time, which when you think about it, is a lot better than no children at all.

In May of 1998 I started seeing another General Practitioner who also used other therapies where possible as I felt the he might be able to help me, and through his testing he told me a lot of things that were true, even though I hadn't told him anything at all. He told me that the reason why I wasn't getting pregnant was because my ovaries had aged a lot quicker than the rest of me, due to my emotional trauma. He added it was not my fault and I know for a fact he wasn't lying, because as I already said, I had told him very little, except the reason why I was seeking his help. He said that he felt that he could help me, so I thought what did I have to lose by getting help from him—after all, here was my last chance to receive any help, as the clinic wasn't doing anything to find answers to my questions.

At the beginning of June I somehow contracted hepatitis A. I was as sick as a dog to the point of having to hang on to the taps in the shower to stop myself falling over. I was getting very dehydrated due to not being able to eat or drink anything because my liver was so swollen that it was even affecting the way I was breathing. The five days that I was in hospital was one of the worst periods during those whole three years and I didn't know if or when I would be able to go back to the clinic. It did take some time for me to pick up, but thank goodness it didn't do any permanent damage although I did find out later that your liver function is meant to be around 55 and mine had reached 2000. No wonder I felt so rotten. We will never be sure just how I contracted Hepatitis A but there were two possibilities. I either picked it up at Mum's sister's funeral from a cup of tea and biscuits which, as luck would have it, was on my birthday and a big wakeup call in regards to my own mortality—sitting there looking at a coffin at the same time as trying to deal with the possibility of never having children and knowing one day that coffin would be mine on my birthday. The other possibility was that one of the little girls we fostered might have been carrying the virus. Their father was using drugs, and it was explained that the children didn't have to be sick, they could simply be the carriers of the virus. The most annoying thing out of this whole horrible mess was that the children's social worker would not allow the doctor to take blood samples to check out which child might have been infected. This didn't make any sense to me, and I put it to them that any future foster parent had the right to know so they could be extra careful. Later in the year the girls did move on, which in some ways was a relief because their father had given us a strong signal of his intention to shoot us! We ended up having to get the police involved because Ian didn't even know what he looked like and we had no idea if we were being watched. However, I did miss the girls and it took a while to get used to the fact they had gone and weren't coming back.

At last September came and I just knew that I had to go for one of my last trips to Adelaide. I couldn't put it off for ever and like I said to my local doctor, I was almost too scared to go in case it didn't work, but then again, if I didn't go, then it never would. I took the same amount of Clomid again and I was just hoping that it gave me the desired result. I felt horrible going to the city and I would have turned back if I hadn't taken the drugs. I knew that this was my second to last trip regardless of what happened.

This time it took a lot out of me as I hardly ate at all, I simply wasn't hungry. This wasn't normal for me, but I did go to the show for a few hours just to pass the time, but I didn't really enjoy it because it was mainly designed for children, the one thing that I was struggling to get. As least this time we struck gold regarding getting my daily blood samples, which are required for measuring the hormones to see just how close I was to ovulation in my cycle. Andrea (my nurse) and I were really pleased. On the Monday I went to see the G. P. /naturopath for a check up and guess what? He was willing to do a blood test that I had requested from my local doctor. The test picked up what I had thought, and that was I had a progesterone deficiency. I went and bought some cream that hopefully would help in getting all of my hormones back to normal.

The day before the scan I went to the toilet and to my horror I noticed spotting, which for me was totally abnormal. In all of my 25 years of having periods I had never spotted in this manner before. On Thursday I had a scan which showed that I only had one large follicle and two smaller ones on the right side, which indicated to me that the drugs didn't have the same effect as last time I tried, which was disappointing. I don't think it reached the 1000 mark. I was inseminated with the donation on Saturday and Sunday and then I just had to wait. When Kerrie did the insemination on Saturday, she mentioned to me that my cervix looked a bit rough and it bled when it was touched with the suction tube, which in itself wasn't normal, or was it? I was going to have it checked out as I didn't want to die of cervical cancer. I wasn't expecting the insemination to work, because I had been through so much in the past three years, it's not funny! I went and visited most of my friends who had been very supportive during the past three years because to me they were very special.

One horrible comment was made to me by a woman who was expecting her third child, her words of wisdom (I'm being sarcastic), were that there must be a reason why I wasn't meant to have children. I found that very hard to swallow as I couldn't work out why people who don't have to struggle to get their children, feel they have the right to be so judgemental regarding those who simply don't have any control whether or not they can conceive.

On Saturday afternoon I went and had afternoon tea with the rest of my Donor Conception Support group and I found them to be very supportive because we all had the same issues and concerns. By the end of the year there would be three families with children which was very encouraging because it showed me that it does work for most, so I had to hope that I was lucky enough to be given the greatest gift of all.

I went home on the 13th September, doing everything to avoid thinking about my prospects of getting pregnant as this had been my second to last trip to Adelaide, but sure enough, five days after returning home I started to feel sick for no apparent reason, and had more frequent urination, which became frustrating after a while simply because I didn't know the cause of it. As much as I was trying to convince myself that I wasn't pregnant, I felt I couldn't face the disappointment of it not working. I had this dream which was so vivid it wasn't funny, and in the dream it HAD worked and I was going around telling all of my special friends that it had worked and their faces lit up like Christmas trees.

On 26th September my heart sank as I got what at first seemed to be a period, but it wasn't normal as it wasn't flowing as usual. The discharge was quite brownish and the only way which it was coming out was if I wiped out the opening with toilet paper. I wasn't feeling a hundred percent, but I thought it was because I was upset. After all, I only had one more chance for ever.

When I woke up on Sunday morning, I felt a pain go across the bottom of my stomach and that's when I realised this wasn't normal because out of nowhere there suddenly appeared bright red blood which seemed to stop as quickly as it began, then went back to a brownish discharge with still no proper flow. The next time I went to the toilet it had changed again and it was now a deep crimson red which really freaked me out. I had never had a cycle like this in my life. On the Monday I went to the doctor to find out what was going on as I needed some clarification of what had happened. I knew it wasn't normal. She was pretty tactless and told me that it seemed a pregnancy had started, but for some reason didn't continue and then she told me that fifty percent of pregnancies ended like this. I knew this was not totally true and for the first time I stuck up for myself and said to her that it doesn't do anything for me does it? I got the impression that she didn't like my comment too much and another thing which really bothered me was her attitude about my cervix concern. She just simply said there's nothing we can do about it and that it was normal for it to bleed, how would she know as she didn't even suggest a smear test to check for any abnormality.

I was talking to a friend regarding my visit to the doctor and she, like me, was not totally impressed by what had happened, and she pleaded with me to go to a second doctor, at least to get my cervix looked at and also to clarify what had really happened on 26th September as I honestly believe that I was pregnant, because as I said, it wasn't a normal cycle.

There were other issues that I wanted to clear up, for example, if I was in fact pregnant, I had no idea of what my blood group was or what that of the donor was either, and if I was A positive and he was A negative, would my last chance of conceiving a child be affected because of this? I also wanted to find out if there was anything that could be done to avoid a repeat of what just happened, after all, when I had this last go, it was over forever.

I had my days when I cried a little to myself because I never expected something so horrible could happen so close to the end of my struggle, that of being given my only wish for a whole lifetime. As usual Ian never offered to console me at all, the only comment he made was that some people find it more difficult to get pregnant than others. I found this very hard to cope with as after all, I was his wife! I decided to have a talk with my normal doctor to see what I was supposed to do if my last chance failed. I honestly could not see how I was going to cope with the grieving process by myself because if and when I cried, Ian complained about it. A couple of examples—for instance if I cried when I was in bed, instead of giving me a hug, he would complain that he couldn't get to sleep so then I would feel I had to go into another room so he didn't get cranky with me. Other times if I was upset when he got home from work, he would simply say "I don't know why I come home if you're going to be upset all of the time", so then I felt that I had to leave the house if I wanted to cry, otherwise he would get a bit cranky and of course, that would make me feel worse. I was honestly scared that if my last chance failed Ian wouldn't give me any support and would criticise me for crying and I could end up in the cemetery. A person who has no support can sometimes snap! I believe there's a big difference between planning to kill yourself because you've done something stupid for which you can't handle the consequences, and suddenly snapping permanently because you simply feel that you can't handle any more emotional pain and you can't talk to your companion about the way you feel, it makes you feel as if you have no release valve. I had found it very difficult to cope when I got to the point of being in so much emotional pain that I didn't know what to do with myself and now I realised that this is the point in time when I just wished that I could die as I didn't know what to do to help myself feel better. I just felt totally alone and isolated and I just hoped that I could get some helpful hints from the doctor.

I rang the hospital to find out when they were shutting down for Christmas and to my horror they were closing from 15th December until 26th or 28th January. I really didn't see how they would need that many weeks off as a lot of people would have not had cycles to suit their holiday plans, and hey—it doesn't take that many weeks to clean a clinic, does it? If I didn't go down for my last go that month, I might not fit into the December cycle either because I would be cutting it a bit fine with my timing. I was just hoping I didn't have to wait until February as I thought on the one hand it might be a bit much for me to handle because I wanted it to be over, but then again I might have needed that time to get my body in order so I would have the best chance of getting pregnant.

I decided I needed to go and have a talk to my normal doctor before we left to get some suggestions on how to cope if in fact it didn't work. I honestly didn't know how I was going to cope with the emotional pain without Ian's support and I didn't want to get to the point of losing the will to live because I simply didn't know how to keep going. On 14th

October I went for a second opinion regarding my cervix and I couldn't believe it—for the second time straight I had to push to get a smear test done. I was told again that bleeding from the cervix was normal. I was honestly beginning to wonder what on earth student doctors were being taught in medical school. It was very easy to pick that the doctor I saw was fresh out of school should I say. She tried to tell me that the clinic wouldn't know the donor's blood group—what a lot of rot, it's in their own literature! I didn't get an answer to my blood group concern, but then again I felt I had to prove that I had something wrong before she would even check anything out, she made me feel that she didn't care anyway. When she did finally check, she seemed to take a few steps back mentally, once she realised that I was telling the truth. As to just how many women enjoy fronting up for smear tests, I would say not too many! I had to find out the test results the following week. She sent three test specimens away when normally they would only send one, so as you might imagine, I wasn't coping well at that time. I had taken our names off the available foster parents carer lists because I didn't feel that could give the children my best when I'm not coping myself. Thank goodness Kirsty and Lucy seemed to understand and said they would keep in contact with me to see just how I was going.

When the results did come back, they were all clear, but what made me most angry in regards to the whole thing was the fact that I had to beg and plead to have the tests done to start with. It just made me wonder how many women die because they aren't being listened to until it's too late. At the visit to my normal doctor we had a good chat about my predicament concerning the way I would react if in fact I didn't get pregnant on my very last try. It was totally beyond my understanding why some people in this world don't seem to understand that infertility is a loss, because it never stops affecting your life. It determines how many friends you have, which in turn determines how much social life you have, because as sad as it seems, people who have children don't have a lot in common with those who don't. As I said to the doctor, if you go to the funeral of a relative and show no emotion, you are classed as heartless but yet in our case we were criticised for crying over what most would consider nothing. The doctor agreed to talk to Ian if in fact it didn't work, because in spite of what seemed years of talking, I couldn't get through to him that there was such a thing as emotional pain and that I simply couldn't just turn it off when I wanted to. We set up the appointment just in case it was needed, and I hoped for the best. When it came time to go to Adelaide, I just cried and I couldn't believe I had been through so much and come out with nothing except a broken heart, which I felt could only be mended by one thing—and you know what that was. I definitely was not a happy soul and did very little while I was in the city, as usual it was hard for them to take my blood for the daily hormone testing which in itself only seemed to be adding to the trauma of the whole situation. I couldn't even go to visit my mum this time as I felt that I couldn't handle too much more.

Before my time at the clinic was over I picked up a bug, so of course it was even harder to get blood samples out of me. I was that off that I nearly fainted as well as chucking up at the same time. Poor Kerrie, I really felt bad about it but then again it wasn't my fault. Kerrie was one of the few people I had met in all that time that I truly felt was cut out for this type of work. People who need the clinics are there through no fault of their own so their emotional status isn't too good to start with and a bit of compassion goes a long way. The only good thing about that last try was that I was the only patient going through the clinic because it seemed nobody else's cycle suited their closing date.

On the last day I was there, it was very hard because I knew I would never be returning. Ian had said I was only allowed to have two more tries forever or else I would need a lawyer, and as you can imagine, that sent a terrible chill down my spine. I looked at him in total wonderment, shock and disbelief because the consent form I had didn't run out until February 1999. Maybe I was wrong, but I thought a consent form was equivalent to a promise and it was totally beyond me how someone could break their promise, especially when the outcome would affect the rest of our lives. Saying goodbye to the staff at the clinic was the hardest thing that I had to do, I knew that I had to be very polite to them, even the stupid doctor. I might have had to see him because if I got pregnant I would still need to have contact with the clinic after the baby was born because there was information that they needed to be told so they could pass it on to the donor father. They wished me a Merry Christmas and I simply replied that we wouldn't be having Christmas because I already had a horrible feeling that I would once again come out with nothing, especially after what happened in September. When I got home I simply turned off emotionally so I could not even think about it as I knew there was no point in being upset any sooner than I had to be. We didn't even put up a Christmas tree, I simply couldn't get into the season's spirit.

As you might have already guessed, I didn't get pregnant and to rub it in I got my period on Christmas day. So that was it for me. I didn't tell Ian straight away because I didn't want to ruin his Christmas. I could only keep it from him for a few days because we had to go to the doctor's appointment which I'd already arranged. The closer the time to the appointment, the more distant and numb I felt as I simply couldn't believe that this was happening to me. As luck would have it, on the day of our appointment there were children in the local clinic's waiting room. I felt as if I could cry any minute and even Ian noticed the painful expression on my face and asked if I was in pain. I just said no, it was in my heart. Seeing it was really Ian's appointment, I decided to go outside and sit on the lawn area to get away from the children. I had already told Ian to tell the doctor that I was sitting outside if and when he called me and I wasn't in the waiting room. When it came time to walk into his rooms, it was almost too much for me, it was like going to a funeral but there was nobody to say goodbye to. I was offered a drink of water which I refused, not out of rudeness, but simply because I could only manage to look at the grey carpet. It's very hard to explain, but I just felt motionless and this whole thing was nearly more than I could bear emotionally and physically, in other words, the only thing that I could feel was total despair. I didn't want to have to believe that this was the end of the road for me and I just thought to myself, how on earth did I get to this point and end up with nothing to show for all of my efforts over the past four years? I will never know what was said on that visit to Ian, the only thing I can remember the doctor saying to him was did he understand what had been said to him, and Ian replying yes. To my horror, I was asked by the doctor if I had married Ian just to have children, which took me totally by surprise, even though it was a question I had been asked time and time again by Ian. I thought he was feeling very insecure and just needed to know whether or not I would leave him if there were to be no children. I just simply replied with a very strong "no" which should have given Ian a definite answer.

Because of how I was handling the visit, I was asked if I was feeling suicidal and I just reminded the doctor that I had nearly run the car into a tree a couple of years earlier at a point when I felt that I couldn't take any more. I was put on anti-depressants and also sleeping pills because now I wasn't sleeping at all. The doctor felt that I had depression going by my body language. I had to go back in two weeks to see how I was going with the pills, which by the way were really horrible, when I started taking them I felt so rotten that I was rolling around on the floor which certainly wasn't my normal behaviour. After a couple of days, I felt as if I could almost fly, besides feeling so happy that it was like when Ian and I first got married. I had to see the doctor three times after I started on the medication to let him see how I was going with it, but I really think it was also to simply let me talk because I couldn't talk about my feelings at home and also I was sure that Ian had really learned a lot at his appointment, but time would tell.

The sad part about our visit to the doctor together was that he had to plead with Ian to hug me when I was upset and he made the comment that he would be asking how it was going. This comment made me realise that my observations regarding Ian's lack of compassion were correct and it was not just my imagination. I was feeling bad that my local doctor would be leaving in a couple of months time as regardless of the fact that he was being paid to listen to my problems, caused by my situation, no amount of time or Medicare cheques could buy the amount of compassion this man had shown me over the past few months. With him leaving, it was like my last connection with my infertility struggle and loss of our child that should have been born in June 1999, was being torn away.

Just after Christmas one of my special friends, Helen, sent us a lovely arrangement of flowers and as you might be able to imagine, they meant a lot to me as they were the only ones we got. The flowers meant so much to me that I took about ten photos of them so I could get a decent one suitable for enlargement. I had the photo which I had framed, hung up in the small spare room where mum normally slept when she visited. I also placed a framed copy of the poem I wrote in coming months in the room to match. As you can guess, I cried for the simple fact that someone had taken the time to show that they cared when I felt not too many cared at all. Poor Ian, he couldn't work it out and later that day when we ran into some more of our friends down the street, Ian with his lack of wisdom told them not to give me flowers because they would make me cry. I later found out that they couldn't believe his attitude. I felt it deeply because people in our position have no tangible way of saying goodbye to our dream of ever having a family, which, it seems so many take for granted when they can achieve it so easily. There was no funeral to attend, no tombstone to choose and arrange, and therefore no lasting monument to acknowledge this phase of our life, regardless of the fact that we came out of it with nothing except countless tears, tissues and broken hearts

It was about this time that the beginnings of a poem started to come into my mind on a regular basis, I just couldn't get the words out of my head so I decided to try and work on the rest of it because I knew it would be the only tangible piece of evidence I would have in connection to our struggle to have a child, which was denied me, and I would never know why.

How do I get to say goodbye When you never came? You
sent a message to my heart To tell me you were on your way.

When I began to feel your presence I didn't know
what to say As after all, you were a gift The most
precious of gifts that could come my way.

Before I understood it all Our time together had
passed And you my precious Had gone up to the
great beyond And become a shining star.

My empty heart Looks to the sky at night And wonders,
what would have been As In my eyes You were the
most precious gift That had even been given to me.

Now there was nobody at our local medical clinic that would have full understanding of the emotional hell I had been going through for the past 4 years. I could only hope that whoever I got to choose as my new medical professional would have some understanding of why I was taking anti-depressants and the occasional sleeping pill. Suddenly I had no sense of direction. I had never had my own mother, and I could never be a mother either, so now I had no idea of what I might want to do, if and when I did anything at all. I had been told that the grieving period could take up to two or three years but I failed to understand just how something like that which could affect the rest of my life could be adjusted to in a couple of years. I guess it depended on the individual person. Suddenly about a hundred and one things seem to hit me in the face at once, things which I had to deal with, yet I had no idea of how and if I would deal with any of these issues. There seemed to be so many, to the point that it was almost overwhelming beyond anyone's ability to cope.

In February 1999 I had started a baby-sitting job, looking after another little boy who had only just had his first birthday. Much to my surprise, I coped quite well with the fact that I was minding a baby when I had only recently found out that I would never have any of my own. I was still taking my medication, but by early April I was starting to get pain on the same side as my liver, so I ended up going back to the doctor to find out what was going on. A blood test revealed my liver was being affected by the pills and we could only assume it was as a result of the hepatitis A in June 1997. So that was the end of the anti-depressants.

Not long after this, we received a letter from the Reproductive clinic, the first clinic we had attended, advising us that now there was a specialist coming to our local area on a monthly basis. After thinking about this for a while, I suggested to Ian that maybe, just maybe, we could go and see if the visiting specialist would be able to help in some way, as now we would not have to travel to Adelaide. Much to my surprise, Ian agreed and as far as I was concerned, I had nothing to lose. We finally had our first appointment in July and it was agreed that I would do what is known as the G. I. F. T. program. I had never had a full stimulated cycle before, most likely because we couldn't afford it—it costs $500, even if you have a Healthcare Card. I got really excited as I thought to myself that I had a real chance. Apart from having the needles for nearly three weeks, the worst part of the whole thing was chucking up after the general anaesthetic. The procedure made my stomach pretty sore, I had had my navel cut so the eggs and sperm could be placed into my right side fallopian tube. Strangely enough, two days after it was done, I got the horrible feeling that it hadn't worked, simply because I didn't notice any physical difference or subtle changes which I had noticed when I got pregnant previously. Well, I was right in thinking that it hadn't worked as I was definitely not pregnant, much to my disappointment, and I know it really affected Ian, even though he didn't say a lot.

The procedure had taken place in September 1999, and I thought that I might have the remaining embryos put back just before Christmas. I wanted to use them before we received a $200 storage bill. When I rang the clinic to put my name down for my try, I asked if they were going to do anything different in the second part of my cycle, as I had just had a 40 day space between periods. The nurse simply said no. After all I had been through, this set alarm bells ringing instantly and I told them that I had just changed my mind and would not be coming in before Christmas. I now began to suspect that I was not being told the truth. There had to be something wrong and somehow I had to prove it before it was too late for me to achieve our goal of being parents. I had no idea of just how long Ian would let me go to the clinic after what I had just been through. It turned out that I wouldn't have the remaining embryo transferred until July 13th, 2000. I decided to do some of my own blood testing while there were no drugs in my system, the only way to get a correct reading. I had been very lucky that my new doctor was willing to go along with the idea. I had started using the progesterone cream in February 2000 and at the same time that month I had a 28 day blood test done to see what was happening in the hormone department and to my horror, it showed up what I had long suspected, I had been told the biggest lie one could be told by a fertility specialist!!

I didn't have a hope in hell of ever getting pregnant, let alone staying that way for the whole forty weeks. The blood tests proved that I was not producing enough progesterone to assist with ovulation, let alone support the development of an embryo for the following three months until the placenta could produce enough progesterone by itself. It is impossible for me to describe how I felt as I had trusted these people, only to find out that they had done the cruellest thing that could have been done to a person in my position. I found out that I should have been given progesterone pessaries for the second half of my cycle after an embryo transfer. I didn't even know that these pessaries existed, so as you would understand, there is no way for me to put on paper just how I felt. I was unable to comprehend how one human being could do this to another. Regardless of my local doctor advising our specialist of my hormone problems which they should have already corrected, they chose to ignore it and hadn't helped me with my problem. I will never understand how three doctors who I had, up until then, felt they had the right to deny Ian and me the best chance possible to be parents. I couldn't explain if I had to, just how I felt when I realised how much I had trusted these people, only to find out that I could never trust anyone one hundred per cent, because you never know what it might cost you until it's too late.

If it had not been for one of our friends who just happened to be a midwife, we would never have found out how all of my hormones worked, and more importantly—where we could get help, seeing none was forthcoming from the clinic. I finally managed to get my hands on some four percent progesterone cream and surprise, surprise, my cycles became one hundred percent better. I was now pretty sure that I had never been fertile up to this point, otherwise we would have had children years ago. I felt totally elated in May when the blood testing showed for the first time that I had ovulated without drugs and my cycles were now in normal range instead of being anything up to forty days.

I knew that I had been told by some that miracles do happen, but I never thought that this sort of thing could happen to me. As already mentioned, we had the embryo transferred on 13th July and as you can imagine, my hopes were very high that it would work. I was given a support needle at the same time, to give the embryo a good chance of survival, so now we had to just wait and see what the outcome would be. I had ovulated on my own on the 11th, and it showed that the progesterone level was very normal and the blood test reading was 78, three days later it dropped to 74. I was still not too worried as I was using the cream three times a day believing it would be enough. My next period was due on the 24th, but it didn't show up and I was feeling sick and my chest was very painful, totally abnormal for me.

On the 25th, I felt major pain go across the bottom of my stomach and thought that this must be the end of it all again, but I still didn't get a period. I did notice however, a slight bleed, but it wasn't the same as period blood. Also it wasn't normal for intercourse to be painful, so I went to my local doctor as I thought I might have had the flu. I had a cough with it and I didn't want to get a chest infection. The doctor didn't want to give me any medication as he thought that the signs were too promising and after checking me out, he found the bleeding was coming from the side wall of my vagina and my cervix was closed, so you can imagine what was going through my mind. On the 27th I started losing blood more rapidly and I knew that there was no way any pregnancy would or could survive. The doctor spoke to me that night and told me to have a blood test the next morning to see if there was any pregnancy hormone remaining.

I wasn't very happy now as my hopes had been so high and now they had been crushed. Not long after the blood test was done I had to take painkillers because the pain was very severe. A large piece of tissue was pushing its way through my cervix which was still closed. When the test results came back it showed that indeed, I had been pregnant. My specialist notified me of this only to turn around and deny it at my next visit with her. At that stage I decided to dig my heels in as I had been through enough. So I simply said that I wasn't going to deny my body signals, effectively shutting her up. Fortunately it didn't take too long for my cycles to return to normal, but sadly, emotionally, I couldn't even cry. I can't even start to describe how it felt when I wasn't believed by the very people who were meant to be helping me.

Their main excuse was that it was the side effects of the drugs, but I knew in myself that I had had enough drug cycles to be able to tell the difference between when nothing had happened and when I had been pregnant. I felt that the greatest pain on an emotional level was being caused by the simple fact that there would never be any clinical acknowledgement of the babies I had lost.

About 18 months earlier I decided that if I was to end up with no children, then I needed to have something to look forward to, simply to keep my alive. I knew from previous experience that if I ended up with nothing, I would most likely feel as though I was falling into a bottomless pit, and with Ian the way he was, I didn't know just how I would be able to survive if I had nothing to hang on to. So I put my name down to be an Olympic volunteer, even though I had never really expected I would be accepted. To my amazement I was chosen, and as September drew nearer the more excited I was. I couldn't believe my good fortune. I had to go to Adelaide for an orientation, so we knew what we would be doing once we were allocated our roles. I ended up going to Sydney on the Indian Pacific train, which wasn't too bad except next time I will get a bed! My carriage was full of volunteers who had already been given their security passes which looked like oversized dog tags. I was very fortunate to be able to stay with my brother-in-law who lived at Richmond, so I was able to catch the train directly to Homebush where the main Olympic events were being held. A few days before the big event, I got to go and be fitted for my uniform which was provided free. I was given two sets, so at least I could have one for back-up. My oversized security pass allowed me as a volunteer, free public transport all over Sydney which was great and I enjoyed travelling into the city centre and I just loved going to Circular Quay to watch all the ferries and all the different types of people who had come from all over the globe. I could just sit there for hours on end as I truly felt that this was one of the best experiences I had had in a long time, besides going over to Canada. It truly opens one eyes as to just how the rest of the world can mix in harmony for one cause. I witnessed some very talented people who should have been totally proud of their achievements.

My job description was Spectator Services Host, in the hosting department and that meant helping people with all their questions. One day a workmate and I had been given the job of directing people to the trains. The trains only travelled east or west and a lot of tourists didn't know which train to catch to the city centre. Try to imagine yourself sitting up on a high tennis chair talking with a loud speaker, advising people walking towards you by the hundreds, which line to join. Then the public announcer suggested that the visitors should thank the volunteers. Every time this was suggested, I noticed a Cadbury's show bag coming our way and I quickly added to my speech that all donations of chocolate would be very much appreciated. To my surprise it actually worked, and we lost track of the number of times we were given chocolate and we made sure none of the other volunteers saw what we were doing.

Much to my horror, I was criticised by some people for going to Sydney, these people had families and I didn't, so I figured if I couldn't have children then I could do other things. I didn't understand why some people were so narrow-minded, after all I was helping a great cause. I had bought a couple of tickets to events which were well worth watching and then the night before the Closing Ceremony, word went around amongst the volunteers that there would be a line up for a limited amount of giveaway tickets to the Ceremony. I decided it was a must have, because I knew the tickets were worth well over $1200 each. The morning of the line up I caught the train in at 4am so I didn't miss out. When I arrived you should have seen it. There were those who had slept there in sleeping bags, but even so when the people in charge came around to give us our line number, it was already over number 700 by the time they got to me, so try to imagine all of us waiting around before the sun was even up—but I got a ticket. After I had done my work shift, I went back home for a sleep because I knew I would be home very late. Finally the ceremony was on and there were heaps of people offering good money for any ticket at all, and even though it was very tempting, I decided not to sell my ticket because I had worked for two weeks without pay, so I had really paid for it. I didn't realise it straight away, but they began to put all of us into one big section. The whole evening was totally amazing and finally it was time for the speeches. When it came time to thank the volunteers it seemed like the whole stadium clapped for us and everyone in our section stood. I know it might seem rather selfish, but for me this was a totally amazing moment in time when people actually appreciated what we had done, and what I alone had achieved. It was what I had gone to Sydney to do and I threw myself into the spirit of the event. The next day it was time to catch the train home again and back to reality. In some ways it was quite sad as it was only then that I discovered why there was never any money in our bank account while I was away. Ian in all of his meanness had decided not to bank any of his pay while I was away, so I found myself having to live off my credit card once my spending money had run out. I will never understand why on earth he felt that he had the right to leave me financially stranded while I was interstate, and for a long time I felt totally horrible that I couldn't give any money to my brother-in-law for letting me stay there, after all, they didn't have to. We decided to have another go for sure, and that was that I would make it up to him when I could as I could never do to someone what Ian had done to me.

We decided to have another go at embryo transfer in November and after being a pin cushion for a couple of weeks, the egg pick up was done on 21st November. The drugs were at a higher dose this time which didn't really worry me apart from the fact that my stomach swelled up and I got tired more easily. When I had the day 9 scan to check just how many follicles there were I wasn't happy at all because it only showed three, which did not make much sense considering I was using more drugs. At the same time I thought that it might have been because I was on a different one to when I had the G. I. F. T. procedure. I was quite surprised when I woke up after the egg collection to see the number seven written on the back of my hand, which meant that seven eggs had been recovered, so once again I just had to wait. The next day I checked to see just how many eggs had been fertilised, only to find out that one out of the seven had made it, so I was quite disappointed, but still happy to have a chance at being a mother. At the embryo transfer I was lucky enough to be talking to one of the lab technicians who told me that if nothing happens, you don't feel anything. At this stage I didn't take a lot of notice as I had just had a look at our future child with the help of a very powerful microscope and it was all pretty amazing. Prior to this transfer I had managed to find a doctor who was willing to help me out by giving me a prescription for the pessaries, behind the stupid specialist's back, so I started using 2 per day as I thought it may be enough, but I was wrong.

I had the first blood test taken as late as possible on the Friday night before the courier collected it will all of the other samples taken at our local clinic, as this was just over 24 hours since it had been placed in my uterus. I didn't expect the hormone to be very high. When I rang for the result, I couldn't believe my luck.

The reading was 206, and this was the highest it had ever been in all of the years of trying and it proved to me that I definitely had been suffering from a lack of progesterone.

On the Saturday afternoon I suddenly got this weird feeling in and around my uterus and then I suddenly remembered what the nurse at the hospital had told me and I thought, could I be this lucky? Four days after this stunning result I had another blood test done and guess what! It was now 343. My next cycle was due to start on 7th December, however four days before this I did notice that my body signals had changed from what they were usually. My period was two days late and on the 7th, my progesterone level was still 30. As far as I was concerned, if I wasn't pregnant, the hormone level would not have been that high, it would be zero. On the 9th the bleeding started, but it was not normal to the point where it was the colour of watermelon juice and had a completely different consistency. There also appeared large clot-like features which I could only assume were fragments of the embryo. The second day came with very strong cramping, which certainly wasn't normal for me. For some unknown reason, my period then stopped as suddenly as it had begun. Yet, on the 16th, it started again and I was not feeling very well, so I went back to see the doctor on the Saturday morning. He suggested that all of the product of conception might not have expelled itself. Sure enough, 90 minutes later, another piece of human tissue was expelled and the discharge stopped.

As you can imagine, Christmas was the last thing I wanted to cope with that year, as to me it mainly revolves around children. Ian couldn't work out why I was looking sad as to him; nothing was missing regardless of what I had told him. Just before the end of the school term we took in another two foster children, Zac aged 9 and Dale aged 7. I was quite happy for them to go to their grandparents for access visits, sometimes I found it very hard to make out as if nothing was wrong for the sake of everyone else in the house.

2001

By now I was thinking seriously about dumping my current specialist because I was far from happy with her attitude. I made up my mind to see if I could get in to see the professor, as I had heard very good comments about him and I felt the way things were going that I didn't have anything to lose. I had a good talk to one of the nursing staff who arranged to have my clinical notes moved without me ever having to see my old specialist again. What a relief!

Finally my appointment came around on 28th February and my first and main impression was that I was being spoken to and not at, which was totally different to what had happened in the past. I could hardly believe the difference in the attitudes of the two specialists and I would have been quite happy to talk to this new one all day. I was very surprised with his very gentle nature and his sense of commitment for his work. It was very noticeable that he really wanted to give us the best chance of being successful. I had no idea of the surprise that I was going to get as a result of my next visit. After I had given the professor my views and he had given me his in return, he simply asked me why we had the current donor, Mr YH and my reply was that it just happened. I was then informed that Mr YH was only half as productive as the original donor, Mr QE. As you might imagine, I could not believe what I had just heard and I instantly began wondering if this was the reason why I only had one egg to fertilise. I now used this opportunity to get his opinion on micro injections, which the last specialist had said I couldn't have because I was using donated gametes. Well, was I in for another surprise. He simply said to me that we don't normally use this procedure with donated sperm, but he would allow me to try it next time and the technique would be used on half of the eggs collected. Apart from being very pleased with the fact that I was being given a chance I'd been waiting for in the past, I couldn't believe the extent of the lies I had been told by the last specialist. My honest opinion is that they hadn't cared at all if I had a child or not, and as far as I was concerned, they should not have been dealing with people in our position. After all, people like us went to them for help!

The professor and I agreed to do what is called a 'flare cycle', in short I would start using the drugs from day 1 of my cycle, and in an ideal world it would all go well. Well, in the scheme of things as far as my luck ran, that never happened. I started the next dose of drugs on the 21st march after having a blood test done which proved I didn't ovulate, and that was no real surprise. Another blood test and scan was done on the 27th, six days later and as well as showing that I had a cyst, the progesterone level was still 33, so that cycle was cancelled. This didn't really bother me too much as I knew that the consent form didn't run out until August that year so I felt I had plenty of time up my sleeve. I was told to phone on day 1 of my next cycle to book in for another try with hopefully better luck this time. I was to have a scan on day five or six. That cycle was quite strange as well as the last one, and had only gone on for 13 days which certainly wasn't normal in anybody's books.

As luck would have it, my next cycle started on the same day as the cyst ruptured and on 1st April (April Fools Day!) while we were 90 kilometres from home, so I was not entirely happy about it. We had taken the two boys to the movies and McDonalds for lunch. I did go and have the scan done on 5th April, which showed that I still had old follicles remaining from my last cycle, so when I rang for the results; I was given permission to have a trigger needle to rupture them. I wasn't feeling very good due to the hormone imbalance. I went to my local clinic and asked for the needle to be given as it was the one thing I couldn't do, and that was put a needle into my own stomach. I honestly have no idea how drug addicts can do it, day in and day out for years on end.

The nurse wasn't satisfied with my explanation because I had no paperwork to prove it, because I was told on the phone only minutes before I arrived there. She went off her rocker. I was really peeved with her high and mighty attitude and I told her to call the clinic herself if she didn't believe me. I also gave her a speech on how I felt about the way I was being treated. I got the impression that it didn't go down too well, but I had gotten to that point because I had been through so much rubbish. I had just about had enough and I wasn't going to take it anymore when it wasn't of my doing. So, the clinic was phoned and a piece of paper was faxed through stating that the needle was in fact meant to be given to me, as I had politely requested in the first place. But then there was one slight hiccough that I must not forget to mention, which actually was quite funny from my point of view. There was no doctor on duty at the clinic to sign the needle order form, which made the fax worthless and a thorough waste of everyone's time. I did not dare let the nurse see me smile, because by now she was on the verge of boiling and almost having a stroke! She was now on a mission to find a doctor who would be able to verify the fax as she was still not convinced that she could legally give the needle. Personally, by that stage, I felt that it should be shoved up her rear end which might have helped deflate her ego, which was now past a joke. She did find a doctor and luckily for me he was very calm about it and took it in his stride. After she had been rude enough to hold a little talk with him behind closed doors, finally the needle was given to me by the doctor himself, which was actually a bit of relief. It was very obvious to me that he clearly understood my position and he fully understood why I needed the needle, especially after I had explained the day's events. I was however bulk-billed to cover the cost of the phone call, which to this day I regard as very childish on the part of the nurse, because after all, I do employ the doctors there as I had been there with health problems in the past few years, and they earned their fair share from seeing me.

I ended up going back on 11th April as I now had an infection in my cervix. I can only put that down to the cyst rupturing by itself on 1st April, but it wasn't really very good as I couldn't sit down or walk around very much at all. I was now starting out on what was to be one of my regular high doses of antibiotics. After this was over, I was just beginning to think that things would return to normal and I had another blood test done on the 19th and it showed that the hormone was five. I then had another sample taken on the 24th and it showed that as far as the hormones were going, they really weren't going anywhere. So on 3rd May, I went down to the reproductive clinic to have another scan and surprise, I now had a cyst on my left ovary. The last one had been on the right side.

I was in for yet another surprise, the two nurses just smiled at me and soon enough I had one of the doctors sitting by me telling me what would be happening next, the cyst would have to be drained via my vagina. He explained that he could do it in the scan room as it was only a fifteen second job, but the nurses don't like it being done that way, so he said he would take the more humane approach and do it in theatre once I had been given a bit of anaesthetic. It all hit home when he said to me "see you in theatre tomorrow". At that point I just felt blown away because I had only just come down for the day trip. It was quite a shock to me as I had no idea that anything was really wrong, except I had noticed a bit of pain on my left side, but I thought it might have been imagination, considering all the things which had happened to me in the past.

When I'd left Helen's place that morning, she said good-bye and the thought never occurred to me to call her at work to ask if I could sleep over again, so I ended up staying the night across the road at the retirement village. Ian had no idea that anything was wrong with me, and I had to let him know. When I called, the answering machine wasn't on, so I had to call one of my friends at home to ask if they could leave a note for Ian explaining why I wasn't coming home. After an unplanned shopping trip, I settled in at the retirement village for the night. I had been told that I couldn't have anything to eat or drink after 4am on the day of the procedure, so I lay down just before 5pm to have a short sleep. I was quite tired, which I now realise was most likely because of my hormone imbalance. I had intended to get up and have tea with the residents, until I woke up and realised it was past 10pm. My stomach just sank because I thought to myself, what have I done now? There was only one option left and that was to go back to sleep and avoid the misery of an empty stomach. I was quite relieved when the morning came and it was time to walk across to the hospital. I was thinking that this would be quite simple, as not much could go wrong here. Seeing I wasn't feeling or looking really sick, I could see the funny side of it now, but I thought maybe I should apply for a job on one of the 'soapies', acting as a hospital patient because by now the staff were remembering me from my last visit.

Rumour had already gotten around about my lovely veins, so I just said that I couldn't have good veins as well as a great complexion. I had to smile to myself when the hunt for my veins started as the doctor who was going to drain the cyst was stroking my arm and then he made the suggestion that maybe they could use gas on me and I thought jokingly to myself, boy—you have deteriorated since yesterday. I made the statement that the doctor was just waiting for his 15 seconds of fame. Seriously, this doctor seemed to have the ability to show and treat people with compassion which certainly meant a lot to people in our position. One day, unknown to him, I noticed that when he was walking down the passage towards a patient from behind, he would just simply touch her on the shoulder as he passed her by. This showed me a side of him which couldn't be explained in words. I just wished there were more people like him around as the world would be a far happier place.

While I was waiting in the holding bay before I was taken into theatre, I was provided with a bit of free entertainment. I couldn't believe what I was seeing. There was an elderly lady speaking with her doctor. One normally asks the doctor questions and then gives them time to answer. Well, there was this lady telling the doctor what to do and from what I could gather, she had very bad lung problems because she was checking out her chest x-rays and reading all her reports. The funniest part of all was when the doctor asked where she was from, her reply was that she was from Coffin Bay and my immediate thought was boy, she will soon have one of her own (meaning her coffin). The lady was so forthcoming with her requests, and I thought to myself, gee lady, I was told to be here and you're telling the doctor what you want!

As for the draining of the cyst, it went well and by the way, before I forget, when I woke up from the anaesthetic after it was done, I couldn't believe what I saw, there was that same lady, sitting up reading her notes, yet again! The doctor came to visit me and said I had to have a blood test again on the 10th May to check if things had gone back to normal. Well, nature beat everybody and my next cycle started 2 days later, much to my surprise. As this last cycle had been 37 days, I wasn't sure what was going to happen next as most things in life appear to be unpredictable.

As luck would have it, I was in theatre just over two weeks later for egg pickup, but this time it was all quite different as it was done on a public holiday and because of this I was actually admitted into the maternity building as the day surgery suite was closed and I was the only having egg pickup that day at this hospital. The great part was the fact that I was given a proper bed in a single room and I thought to myself, I could handle this every time—no worries. After having the eggs picked up and I was awake enough to enjoy it, I was given a lovely chicken dinner which was a lot better than sandwiches and juice. I was very happy as they had picked up five eggs and as far as I was concerned, the cycle had been successful as long as I had at least one egg to fertilise. I was granted my wish and found out that on the Tuesday I had one very good embryo to be transferred the next day. I had noticed that I was a bit sore after this pickup, but I really didn't take too much notice and thought nothing more of it. So on the Tuesday night I decided to go out with Helen and her friend. I went to bed not long after we arrived home only to wake up at 1am in severe pain to the point that I chucked up as well as being all bent over and having the shakes. Helen rang up the hospital and explained to them what was going on and they informed one of the current clinic doctors who in turn phoned us. Much to my horror I had managed to wake the professor up and in spite of the fact that I was far from well, I did feel really bad. After I had finished speaking to him, we had decided that unless things got worse we would still transfer the embryo. I went back to bed after taking a few painkillers and hoped for the best.

I did have the transfer done and I was told that it was perfect and only twenty percent of the transfers they do are perfect, so I was really pleased. We decided that the pain had been caused by bleeding from the right ovary which was a result of the egg pick up. I didn't think much more of it, apart from the fact that I still wasn't walking properly. I happily drove home after making sure that I had allowed enough time for my extra progesterone help to be fully absorbed. I had a blood test on 24th May and the result was great—273. I thought to myself, boy! This is even better than last time so I just had to keep my fingers crossed. I kept using the extra progesterone help every eight hours which now meant that I was using three per day and this was obviously helping, as next time I had blood taken on 28th May, it was 390. My period was due on 4th June and I knew that the embryo had definitely embedded itself as I felt it two days after coming home and by that stage of the piece, I was starting to feel sick and there were a few other clues which you don't have if you're not pregnant. However, on 3rd June, disaster struck again. I had a very bad cramp go across the bottom part of my stomach and my heart just sank. But there was still no period on 4th June when it was due. I went and had my blood test which would prove whether or not I was pregnant. I had a bad feeling when I rang up for the results as I thought that I already knew the answer. The progesterone was still 15 when in fact it should have been zero. When I did get my period the next day it was really heartbreaking because everything seemed to have been going so well. I thought that I was in for a real chance that time. By the time poor Zac arrived home from school, my eyes were glassy from being upset and he asked me if I had been working with onions all day. I just replied that my eyes were sore. To me this was one of the hardest moments in regards to the loss because I couldn't let him have any idea of what truly going on.

My condition was obviously not normal, and I was having constant pain on the right side which just happened to be the side that I bled from during and after egg pickup. I went and saw one of the local doctors on 12th June, and I can only describe her politely as being pathetic. I explained to her about the abnormal discharge which was totally horrific, as far as I was concerned the bleed out was no where near normal as it consisted of a large clot like feature which I honestly believe was the embryo and also a piece of human tissue which I can only say resembled transparent skin which was stretchy and it had to be literally wiped out of my vagina because it wouldn't drain out by itself. As you might imagine, this experience totally freaked me out because in between the tears I thought that I must be literally falling to pieces as I had never in my whole life seen anything like it before and I certainly didn't want to see anything like it again.

I explained to her what had happened during egg pick up and she simply stated that I had just been having an early miscarriage and that I should see the positive side of things because I was further along this time than last and the pain I had mentioned was normal. As you might be able to imagine, I couldn't believe what I had just heard. It wasn't so much what she said but the fact that she said it with a smile on her face which I thought was very out of place considering the reason for my visit.

I ended up seeing my regular doctor on 15th June. He just happened to be the doctor on call and he thought that it might have been an infection, I was given some antibiotics. When I went to pick them up, I couldn't believe what I was reading. I was puzzled as to how on earth one is meant to apply a capsule to an infected uterus. I had to ring him up and check that I had been given the right medication. By now the level of pain had risen quite a bit so I took an extra capsule hoping to get a quick effect, but it didn't happen. I knew something was wrong by this stage so I rang Ian at work and told him not to waste any time getting home because I would have to go back to the clinic. When we walked in I just simply said, "could I please see my normal doctor?" They took one look at me and asked if I wanted to lay down, a great option I thought. The nurse checked out some things and when the doctor did some more checking, he decided that I would have to go over to the hospital and be put on a drip because by now I was far from well in anyone's books. I couldn't even breathe in the normal manner let alone walk normally and at this point I was quite sweaty. It wasn't until I got over to the hospital that it started to hit home just how serious it might have been because the nurse was literally waiting for me at the door.

I was quite relieved when I could just lay down and not have to move anymore. With just a little luck on our side, the needle for the drip went in on the first try, but as for my pulse rate, it had lost the plot and was racing at 140 a minute. I must have looked a total wreck. My stomach was so distended and Ian said to the doctor "can't you just deflate it with a pin?" I felt the doctor was horrified by Ian's comment and he quickly stated quite clearly that it was serious. After doing more checking of my condition and find out that the Berri specialist wasn't home, the doctor informed us that I would have to be sent to Adelaide by Air Ambulance because he now suspected an ectopic pregnancy, even though I explained that I thought I had already expelled the embryo, but an ectopic pregnancy is very, very serious in deed. We had to wait just over an hour for the plane to arrive at our local Airport because it was just coming back from another call elsewhere. While we were waiting I developed the shakes and I was given morphine for pain relief in half doses, because no one knew how I would react to the drug. The reproductive clinic was contacted but there were no doctors on duty so it was suggested that I be sent to the Women and Children's' Hospital. Ian went home and grabbed a few things for me and also brought Zac and Dale to say goodbye. My friend Janet also called in while we were waiting for the plane to arrive.

By that stage I had gone into shock and the morphine had gone straight to my head to the point that when Ian suggested that a couple we knew were down at the hospital already and that they might be able to visit me, I simply replied that they might forget who I was. The trip to Adelaide was not too bad in between dozing on and off with the sound of the plane engines. The nurse who was looking after me asked me very nicely what had gone wrong. When I told her she just said "do you realise that some people cannot have children?" My heart just about melted completely as by now I felt that I had been through so much in such a short time and I didn't even really have enough time to cry. I must have been pretty dopey, I didn't even notice when we landed at Adelaide Airport and asked what the bright flashing lights I could see out of the window were. The nurse explained it was the ambulance waiting to pick me up and that I would soon be in hospital. By now I was past caring because I had no idea of what was going to be done to me. I did see the registrar who had spoken to the doctor in town and he did his own checking, and I mean checking! I had to have an internal examination which I wouldn't forget in a hurry. I also had a scan which showed that I had a couple of fibroids on the outside of my uterus, but apart from that there was nothing to see. I was seen by another doctor also and after a brief discussion he just said to me "I think the best thing we can do is admit you." I thought to myself, I have been flown 200 kilometres from home and I am certainly not going to sleep out in the gutter. Before I was taken to my room, I was taken for another scan as they needed to know whether or not I did have an ectopic pregnancy, because if I did I would need immediate surgery. Fortunately for me I didn't have the baby growing in the tube, so in one sense that was a relief.

Apart from showing up a couple of small fibroids, there was nothing apart from my bladder which was completely full because I was so sick as well as being full of morphine, I didn't have the urge to go to the toilet.

This was probably a blessing as I had no idea on earth how I would have gone on the plane. About midnight I was put on three different lots of antibiotics which all added up to 2000 milligrams per day and yet strangely, three days before (according to the stupid doctor), there was nothing wrong with me. I thought to myself in regard to the stupid doctor at home, that one day someone would die because of her.

By the morning I was feeling quite ill and I think part of it was because of all the medication that was going through my system. Ian came down to the city the next day and stayed at mum's place and they came to see me that afternoon. I still had no idea what else would need to be done to me because the doctor who admitted me had only seen me for a short time. By the next morning I got the feeling that I would be going home soon and sure enough, one of the gynaecologists who I hadn't met before, came to discharge me and he had a nice talk with Ian and me. He explained that he believed that the embryo would have been killed by the infection, which I was a bit relieved to hear in one way, as I thought to myself, well it does make sense to me simply because of the way things happened. I was sent home with three different lots of antibiotics so it goes to show you that I was very sick indeed. I took me a few weeks to get back to normal physically, but as far as emotionally, I simply couldn't let myself even think about it as to me, it was emotional hell. How could I get so close and yet lose it, just before the pregnancy test was done? Regardless of what others might think I know for a fact that the embryo died in the second week of the pregnancy which seemed to fit in very well with how an infection works. The infection doesn't show up any symptoms straight away, that's why the embryo continued to live as long as it did. I was very lucky in a way as I have a photo of it in my bible with the last two. I was to take the medication for a couple of weeks and the infection should have cleared up.

When I arrived home I thought things couldn't get any worse, but I was wrong. A week later I managed to roll both of my ankles going down the front steps. I felt totally sick to the bone as well as being in pain. When Ian finally got home after being out with Richard for a bike ride, he took me to the hospital and I ended up having x-rays which proved I didn't break any bones. Regardless of that, I still couldn't walk and I was on crutches for about three days, spending two of those in bed. I was so upset when I had the accident, I just wondered how much more I could take and I made up my mind that the answer was I just couldn't take anymore at all.

When Ian was helping me into the car, he had both doors open and I was so upset that when I went to throw my wallet into the car, I threw it with such force it went straight through the car onto our neighbour's lawn. After a couple of weeks things seemed to settle back to normal and I thought to myself, great! But at the same time, I still felt that something wasn't right because ever since I got out of hospital I had this pulling sensation on the same side as where things had gone so wrong. I put up with it for nearly two months before I complained about it and finally spoke to two of the doctors at the clinic, one who said he thought that it might not have been too much, and the other one who more or less agreed with me about my explanation of the pulling pain. By now I couldn't sit or stand up without discomfort. We agreed that I should have a laparoscope put in through my navel to see what was going on. I had that procedure on 28th August, 2001.

I couldn't believe the amount of pain I was in when I first started to wake up, but I instantly had my answer. I immediately started pulling up my legs because the pain was so bad that even though I had been anaesthetised, I couldn't keep still to the point where I had to be given morphine and they had to support my legs with pillows. I had been right all the time and the next morning I was told that my ovary had in fact been stuck to my pelvic floor. I was actually relieved that they found something because I knew I couldn't have that much discomfort for nothing. Besides being told the results, I was also told that I couldn't have anything done through my navel again because the doctors had so much difficulty gaining access through my navel and it resulted in severe bruising. The local doctor who I had to see every three days for a checkup couldn't believe what he was seeing as I was part of a survey which was to work out which type of stitches were best, as in normal stitches versus dissolving stitches. Without me knowing, I was getting a wound infection which could not have happened at a more convenient time (just joking!).

Exactly one week after my operation, I had an appointment with the professor which had been made three months before and we could not have ever guessed what would happen that day. Ian and I had gotten up early that day to go to town, even though our appointment wasn't until the afternoon. I wasn't feeling too good when I got up and thought I should mention it to the professor that afternoon. While I was in the shower my navel wound split open and the most disgusting green pus that I had ever seen started oozing out. Ian rang our local clinic to get me an appointment with the nurse, but he was told that we could not be seen until 2pm and then he had to explain what had happened and I was seen about an hour later. The nurse put on another dressing, which only just lasted until we got to our appointment, it was now full of horrid green pus. Luckily for us the doctor who had done the operation was called in and he attended to my wound, only to discover that I had gotten an infection from the hospital, so now I was put on my third lot of antibiotics in less than eight months. We agreed with the Professor that I would, and should, have a break until the beginning of the new year, meaning 2002. As we left, I was patted on the shoulder and he said he hoped we would have a nice Christmas. We had already booked our seats with Qantas to go to visit Ian's family, I had decided I was sick of staying home alone for Christmas as we had no family where we lived. Besides, I hadn't been back since we were married and I wanted Ian to be able to see both of his grandmothers who were well over 90 and in reality, no one knew just how long they had left with us.

We left on 23rd December after attending my cousin's daughter's wedding the day before. The worst part of that was the fact that we only got about four hours sleep because the reception was just too good to leave and we had to be at the airport at 5.15am ready to fly out at 6am. The plane trip was quite good except for Ian laughing like a hyena because he was watching a movie, and at the same time driving me crazy. I could have killed him and diced him out of the window without a second thought. We finally arrived in Brisbane and boy oh boy! Did we ever get a major climate shock. I had never felt humidity like that before in my life. Thank goodness we had worn our cooler clothes, otherwise we would have melted. After we left the airport, we went by the sky train into the main city terminal because we had to get on the tilt train to take us to Bundaberg. Thankfully it had air-conditioning.

I was still quite peeved with Ian because he was as high as a kite due to the fact that he was actually on holidays. I thought I had to get back at him somehow, and I just had to wait for an opportunity. Once the train got going and we all got settled, Ian dropped off to sleep and then I noticed something that was my golden opportunity. The train had an engine carriage at both ends, so that it could change directions anytime it needed to. It also had a television monitor which showed just where we were on a map. As luck would have it, it stated how many kilometres we had to travel to Brisbane, so when Ian woke up I told him that the train had turned around and was going back to Brisbane. The expression on his face was priceless, he actually believed me and went straight to ask the train attendant who told him the same thing. It was so funny because it caught him by surprise. The rest of the trip was uneventful and besides waiting for almost two hours for our lunch to be served, it was quite comfortable. When we did get to Bundaberg, George (Ian's dad) and his sister and kids were waiting for us. The train was slightly late because of a hold up with a passenger who had to switch trains and return to Brisbane. My memory as far as Bundaberg goes was quite good, seeing I had only been there once before. We were quite relieved to finally arrive at Ian's parent's place, as (silly me), I was looking forward to decent air-conditioning. How wrong could I have been?

When we arrived at Ian's parent's home, I was in for a shock. There was no air-conditioning, no ceiling fans and worse still the house was built out of brick, so the best way to describe it would be to call it a rather large sauna. My sweat glands were working overtime, and as a result I couldn't sleep. I reacted so badly to the humidity that I had to take off my wedding ring because my fingers were so swollen. They had never been like that before in my life. As for the rest of our time in Bundaberg, we spent a lot of it looking for cool places to hang out. We ended up seeing more movies in one week than we had seen in the previous four years. We did end up seeing all of Ian's family during the ten days we were there, which was really great as it gave me another chance to get to know them a bit better. It was really good for us to see both Ian's grandmothers again. We left Bundaberg on 3rd January in a hire car which we had for the next three days. We made our way down to the coast to see my former sister-in-law who was holidaying at Caloundra with her two children. It seemed to be a lovely spot for a holiday by the sea with plenty of folks in the holiday mood. We had a lovely time with them all, so I'm hoping it's not another seven years before we see them again. We spent about three hours with her before heading out to Dalby to visit Peter for just under two days. It took a long time for me to adjust to the difference between Peter's first wife and his new partner, I was just hoping that I could get to know her a lot better.

By now we were seriously thinking of leaving Dalby, I had warned Peter that we would be leaving early if they weren't going to be around to spend time with us as there was no point in us being there if they couldn't. The way I think is that when someone travels 2000 kilometres to come and visit you after seven years, I felt they owed it to us to at least be around as much as possible, especially when they'd had four months notice. Peter pleaded with us to stay, so we went out to the Bunya Mountains for the Saturday which was quite relaxing and had beautiful views and great food. Ian decided that he wanted to go for a walk on one of the trails and he lost his bearings until he found someone to ask for directions back to the car park. While he was gone I had a good look around at the shops which had all sorts of things visitors might want. While I was sitting in the car park admiring the different types of birds, I couldn't believe what happened. As always, I was eating squares of chocolate, and this large bird seemed to come out of nowhere and simply took the chocolate from between my fingers, just as I was about to put it in my mouth. No wonder these birds are so good at the game of survival.

We had to get up very early on Sunday for the long drive into Brisbane Airport which turned out to be a total breeze. We didn't even get lost once, so we could enjoy the scenery. We had put over 600 kilometres on the car, which by the way was a late model Ford Falcon, but we were lucky as the hire car agent didn't bother to charge us for it so I thought that was a great ending to our holiday.

The trip to Melbourne took a while, but I didn't mind as I was thinking of all the frequent flyer points I was gaining. We did a quick bit of shopping in the Melbourne Airport because I wanted something to prove that I had indeed been there and in less than 45 minutes we were back in the air to Adelaide, When we landed we went to pick up the car. We had tea with my cousin and his wife before the long drive home. Now it was back to the real world and I knew that we had an appointment to see our local Doctor on the 6th January, to sign a consent form for my last IVF attempt using my own eggs. Ian had been with me at our last appointment with the professor, and we had come to an agreement on what we would do so I had no warning on what was about to happen next. I told Ian that we had to go and sign the forms the next week and he said "do you think it's wise with your problems?" and I said that it was something I needed to do, so that if I came out with nothing that I would know that the result was just the same as last time. This to me was a lot kinder than wondering for the rest of my time if the results would have been different.

Ian came home and got ready to go and I still had no warning of what was going to happen. While we were waiting for the doctor to call us, Ian noticed the papers on the chair next to me and asked me what they were for. I just briefly explained that we were there to sign them. I couldn't go into detail because there were other people in the waiting room. At that point my heart began to sink as I couldn't believe what was happening. It was like a horror movie that I couldn't switch off. Ian said he wasn't going to sign anything. It was like I was being stabbed through the heart. He had told me in September that he would sign it next year, meaning 2002—now, and unless I was wrong, I thought I could believe what he said. To make matters worse, all of this happened less than ten minutes before our appointment, making it too late to cancel anything, even if I wanted to. In a major effort to turn things around I took Ian outside and was very blunt with him. I asked him what was going on and he said he didn't want to sign the papers, so I just had to remind him what he had promised. I reminded him that he had said he would sign them next year, and it was now next year! By that stage I could have cried as I couldn't believe how cruel he was being. I'm the sort of person who if I say something I'm going to do, I keep my promise. Once we made it into the doctor's office, I had to explain why we were there which wasn't easy because I was feeling very tense, not knowing what was going to happen next with regard to Ian's behaviour.

He again said he didn't really want to sign the form because he didn't know if it was right, so I had to jump in and tell the doctor what had transpired during and after our visit to Adelaide, which fortunately left Ian with no choice but to sign. By that stage I felt totally flat because as far as I was concerned, Ian was just being totally childish. What really hurt though, the most though was the fact that the doctor had to alter the consent form to keep Ian happy. When he signed the form Ian was agreeing to one more IVF attempt, and not for twelve months or three more goes, (whichever comes first), which is what the form said originally, and in spite of the fact that I said to the Professor in front of him that I didn't have the right to waste his (the professor's) time if he couldn't help me and as far as I was concerned, I didn't sound like someone who intends to keep trying forever. I couldn't believe how selfish Ian had become, he hadn't been contributing financially for years, so what did he have to lose by just signing a form? I never got so much as a hug when I was very sick, let alone any sympathy when the last embryo died. In fact, just the opposite as I had to keep having sex with him just to keep him happy, regardless of me still losing the discharge from the embryo loss. I just felt cold in my heart and I thought to myself, how could he when he knew what had just happened.

The only way I can sum things up is that Ian had no idea of how to show any compassion and I am in no doubt as to why. Another thing at the visit to the doctor that I found very hard to handle was that Ian stated to the doctor that I frequently spoke about our fertility problems, which was the biggest lie of all. The last time I had spoken about it up to that time was in September 2001 which I thought was very good as one thing I always felt was unfair was that with infertility you are not free to openly discuss your feelings in regards to loss and yet when someone you know dies, you can talk about it for months or even years without being criticised. I just said to the doctor, well maybe I might just have to shut up permanently, so I hope he took it as a warning.

Anyhow, the form was finally signed, but I could have strangled Ian for his childish behaviour. He was exhibiting a different type of thought pattern and I honestly believe that he had had a discussion with his mother because I did notice that the only time I ever tried to bring up the subject of the embryos, she was very chillingly cold. I was prepared to let her have a look at the photo of our last embryo which I had got in the June as I thought that as a grandmother she would be interested to see it. I thought it was a privilege because these aren't the type of photos that you show to everyone. I asked her if she had ever seen a photo of an embryo, half expecting her to show a bit of interest, but I couldn't have been more wrong. The reply was so chillingly cold "yes, I have". I could not believe the response and I hoped that if I pulled off this miracle, next time I hoped that she doesn't turn into a hypocrite because I wouldn't tolerate it. A few days after we had the form signed, I ended up having another scan done because while we had been away, I had had a two week cycle, which is not normal. Sometimes it can be a sign that you might have a cyst and after what had happened last year, I couldn't take any chances because if there was one it would have to be drained before it caused any problems. The result of the scan showed that there was no cyst, but I had a great follicle which measured 21 millimetres and for me, I felt that it was good considering I wasn't on any drug treatment. My next cycle was only 25 days in length, so I thought that I might just mention it to my naturopath, who just happened to be a G. P. as well, which is a great advantage.

On 5th February I had a blood test done to check out my thyroid function because I had shown them the temperature chart I had been doing for the past five months and guess what? My thyroid was not working to its full potential, far from it. It was explained to me that the thyroid works in conjunction with your hormones and if it's not working properly, it would affect your fertility.

Do I need to say more? I felt that we might have finally hit the nail on the head so to speak. But it did raise a lot of questions with regards to the reproductive clinic. I now felt that they relied on the drugs far too much and were not trying to get to the bottom of my problem and they were only worried about the physical condition of my reproductive organs themselves, which doesn't make a lot of sense as each organ works with the assistance of another. I honestly believe that this is why so many couples leave the clinic with nothing but broken hearts and this is truly unfair as those doctors spend seven plus years in medical school learning about the functions of the human body. I started taking capsules which should have helped my thyroid to function correctly.

I had another blood test done later to check how things were going and to my surprise it worked, but not quite fast enough, so I was put on a stronger dose. I now had to take one capsule as it seemed to be working correctly and my body temperature was where it should be at about 36 degrees, whereas it used to be around 34 degrees which was certainly not normal.

On 9th May 2002, I started what was to be my last IVF cycle. It was decided that it would be a flare cycle and this time I was put on 20 units of Lucrin and 375 of Gonal-F per day. As for me emotionally, I had now gone into robot mode. After what happened last year I was expecting to come out with nothing, so basically I just did it again, thinking that the result would be the same as last time. That might sound very detached, but I saw it as a protection device, so that when I got the answer I was expecting, the cruel reality wouldn't be so hard to cope with. On 17th May I had a scan which showed a cyst that measured 49x62x62mm and also a blood test which showed it was not ideal to keep this cycle going, so it was cancelled. I was supposed to have a scan done on day one of my next cycle, to see if the cyst had reduced in size, but I decided that it would be disgusting to be bleeding when I was having the scan, so I decided to have one later. As for the length of my cycle, it was only 13 days in length, so it showed that things were really messed up. I did have a scan done on the 27th at the normal Scanning Department at the Queen Elizabeth Hospital and it showed that the cyst had shrunk, which was no surprise because on the 24th I started getting pain and it lasted until the 26th, and I wasn't feeling good at all. I felt the cyst pop about 8pm on the 24th. As far as I'm concerned, the clinic was very lucky with a capital 'L' that I didn't get an infection as a result of the cyst's fluid going into my pelvic area. Until that day it had never been explained to me why it wasn't drained, as it was quite a bit larger than last year's. When it was finally explained, the reason given was that it wasn't classed as being active, which meant that it wasn't throwing my hormones out of whack. I still believe that with my startling record of mishaps, they should have drained it when it was first discovered.

On 1st June, five days after I had been to Adelaide for the scan, I ended up in the local hospital with severe stomach pain on the right side, the same side as where the cyst was or had been. I had not been feeling very good all day and by teatime I felt totally ill. I was throwing up in the bath as well as having real bad pain at the same time. Ian took me up to the hospital and I just expected to be sent home with pain killers or something. I was in for a shock though, as the 'Doctor on Call' wanted to keep me in because he thought It could have been appendicitis or something similar. I was given painkillers and bowel movement stuff which didn't seem to make a lot of difference so it was decided on Wednesday 5th to send me to the Queen Elizabeth Hospital because I had now been chucking up every 24 hours. The doctor said to me that they felt that I needed to have another laparoscopy to check inside. This was the last thing I wanted because of what happened last time when I was in total agony and got the severe infection in my wound a week later.

I had also been told then that I couldn't have this sort of surgery done again. I packed up all my gear and Ian and I left for Adelaide after I had been given more pain killers and a needle to help me stop feeling sick.

My appointment was for 2pm on the Thursday with a doctor named Ivan. I jokingly said to Ian that I hoped he wasn't Ivan the Terrible, which I could not believe turned out to be so horribly TRUE. To start with, when we got to the clinic counter where I handed in the letter, we were told that they didn't know we were coming and I thought just how stupid did these people think we were? When we finally did get into our appointment, things only got worse. Ivan seemed to totally disregard the letter and stated quite plainly that I wouldn't be having any surgery done even though it had been recommended in the letter. He said he just wanted to send me home with some stronger painkillers, despite the fact that we had just travelled 200 kilometres. He should have been able to see that I was in a lot of pain because by now, I couldn't sit down, let alone stand in the one place for very long. Ian and I had to be very stern with him so he knew we wouldn't be pushed around because by now I could see why some doctors get sued for negligence. He finally agreed that I could go up to the ward to see if there was a bed available for me. We had been told before we left home that there would be one and they managed to get some blood to check for infections and anything else they could think of.

I was told that I would be given painkillers when I got up to the ward but I hadn't been told how they would be given. I guess I just thought it would be by pills or with a needle. I couldn't believe just how wrong I was, when to my horror Ian and mum were sent out of the room and they told me what they had to do. It came as a total shock to me as I had no idea that painkilling medicine could be put up your back passage. The only thing I was told was that all of the mothers who had had caesarean births thought that these were the best things ever. It was nearly too much for me to handle to hear this when I was there trying to have a child via IVF and trying to come to terms with the fact that there was most likely wouldn't be any at all.

I managed to keep my mouth shut as I honestly believed that the nurse didn't mean to be upsetting, but regardless of this I was on the verge of tears because they didn't know but I was meant to be starting my Lucrin needles the next week and here I was, not knowing what was wrong with me and also not knowing whether or not I would be able to start my needles at all. It was very hard to cope when my cycle could be cancelled before it even got started. When there was no chance at home of ever getting pregnant, I got psyched up that maybe this time I would be lucky.

At about 8pm Ivan came in to tell me what would be done to find out what my problem was. I was really disgusted at the thought of IT. I was to have a back passage examination which I thought was totally disgusting. The night before, I was given some pills which were bowel movement softeners, which I didn't think made a lot of sense as I was still going pretty regularly. But I took them anyway just to keep everybody happy. I didn't sleep too well because I was very upset. I had asked Ivan what would happen if they couldn't find out what was wrong with me because I was meant to start my needles the next week and simply, without compassion, he stated that I wouldn't be able to have IVF anymore. That man was very lucky that he didn't get a slap across the chops because by now it was plain to see that he was the Ivan from Hell. I had no idea how on earth he passed his exams to graduate.

The morning came and at 9am it was on. Ivan came in with the nurse who was very nice to me, lucky for him because otherwise he certainly would have copped a mouthful from me. He took some swabs, which by the way I have never been told the results of, so who knows what they were testing me for. Then the unmentionable test was done. He didn't even have enough respect for me as a patient to let me have a sheet over my legs while things were being done and this is when I just saw red. Anyone could have walked in and seen everything I had! Before all of this had started, he had sat on my bed beside me and asked if I had been to the toilet yet, and I simply glared at him and said you're pushing your luck aren't you? He replied that he was only asking, with his ever present annoying smile on his face. After the examination was over, he just left the room without saying anything at all, so I had no idea what was going on. It was very clear that they were trying to chuck me out of the hospital without any explanation of my problem. It was still quite painful and I couldn't walk normally. It was then that Ian and I decided to go up to the fourth floor to talk to one of the reproductive medicine unit nurses, and to tell them what was going on. They suggested that we ask to see another doctor. I was very stern in asking as I didn't want to be put off because I knew something was very wrong. When finally someone else came in, I said that I didn't want to sound ungrateful, but something wasn't right and it was only then that we were told that there was a very stale stool lodged in my bowel. It now all fell into place and I now believe that because of the size of the cyst that should have been drained, all of the stools couldn't get past and as a consequence some was left behind where the bowel was pushed out of shape, and when the cyst finally ruptured, the stool failed to move because it had been there so long. I was just lucky that I didn't get a major infection. The local doctors agreed with my theory, even though the professor didn't but then again he'd been wrong before.

On 19th June I had another scan to check what was going on as the 20th was day 1 of my new cycle. They had taken another blood sample only to find out that it was not quite normal, so some really bright doctor, who I had never met, decided to put me on the pill! Emotionally, this went down like a ton of bricks because this "doctor" should have read through my notes enough to realise that I was using donor sperm because there was no sperm at home. Taking the pill was like putting a knife through my heart and it was really hard to do and I felt that I should have had some choice in the decision. I was to take it until the 12th July after starting Lucrin needles on the 6th. This is what they call a crossover cycle and it was thought that they would have more control of my hormones this way. I went back to the clinic on the 15th for another scan and blood tests, just to see how things were going and on the 19th, I started the Gonal-F at 450mg per day. I continued the needles until the 26th when the cycle had to be cancelled because my progesterone was far too high. I found that a little amusing because I didn't usually have enough in the second part of my cycles. They told me they felt I had already ovulated which really upset me because I had taken the pill and been on Lucrin to avoid this happening. I just cried and wondered why I couldn't ever do a normal first part of an IVF cycle anymore. I honestly believe that I ovulated on the 30th July, the day before the proposed egg retrieval, which still doesn't make any sense because it meant my cycle went on for 55 days, which was outrageous, even by my standards, and to make matters worse, I wasn't feeling too good. I kept sending blood samples until finally on 12th September my next cycle started and I made up my mind that I was going to allow myself to have a normal cycle to let all the drugs out of my system. Besides, I really wanted to do some more blood testing of my own, just using the progesterone cream, to see just how much the hormone was lacking in the second part of my cycle. Luckily for me I was right and the hormone level came in at 4 when it should have been between 12 and 80 and to make things even a bit better, the price had dropped from $200 to $160. My last cycle went for 30 days, so on 11th October I got my hopes up again. I had insisted that this time a scan be done before I started using any of the drugs so as to avoid a cancellation fee which was over $300 once the drugs were started. I wasn't in a position to be able to afford it.

Thank goodness I followed my gut instinct because unfortunately I was right yet again as the scan showed another cyst which was about 5cm in width and held about 80mls of fluid. When I faxed the results to the clinic, I politely made the recommendation that it be drained because I'd had the problem in the past and luckily for me my request was granted and it was drained on 11th October, day one of my next cycle. It was a bit strange having it done by a doctor I'd never met, but he was nice enough and ended up helping find veins which had done their usual thing of being hard to find when they were wanted. I had to see the funny side of it as it's not very normal to have four guys checking out all of your limbs at the same time. As for the procedure, it went well and then I went up to the fourth floor to get the drugs which I would need for my next attempt. I had to start them the next day.

I started on the Gonal-F on the Saturday because they were going to give me a very strong drug to keep my progesterone down once the follicles had reached a measurement of 14 mm. On the 18th October, the cycle was cancelled yet again as the same thing happened. I started using a nasal spray called Suneral and I was to keep using the spray until basically further notice. This time the cancellation wasn't so upsetting because I was halfway expecting it and the professor was very nice to me and I agreed with the reasons he gave. On the way out of Adelaide at one of the last intersections before reaching Gawler, I had to stop and well, you could never guess what happened next, I ended up being along side a hearse with a coffin in it. That in itself is nothing unusual as we all know we are on a one way street, but this time it was very different. I had to look twice to be sure of what I was looking at and much to my horror, it was a little white coffin (no bigger than that of a newborn) with a small spray of flowers on top. Thank goodness I had to concentrate on driving the car otherwise I would have just lost it emotionally. I thought to myself, those poor parents, they must be going through total hell. It made me wonder just how much emotional pain people could cope with when the unthinkable happens. My heart went out to that poor little baby's family and I just hoped that they were being given support. To me, those parents were not that different to me and Ian, except that society now acknowledges the loss of infants and I just hoped that in the near future, people in our position will be shown the same understanding when embryos are lost, because to me they are priceless.

On 1st November I went to Adelaide for the same routine, only to discover that the original cyst had refilled and it was now back to 5cm in width with an extra smaller cyst for company. It was decided that it would be drained on the 15th November if it hadn't gone by itself. My remark to the professor when he said to me that the cyst was back was simply, I don't think it ever left, and it must have started refilling as soon as it had been drained the first time. I also commented that he must be getting sick of seeing me, but he laughed and said "I love seeing you", and I thought, Oh, well fair enough, at least we were getting along alright as doctor and patient and that was what really counted.

Well, so much for me wishing that the cyst would go away by itself, on the morning of the 15th after no breakfast or fluids, it was discovered that it had shrunk to half of its original size however the professor still wanted it to be drained and guess who would be doing the procedure? I never expected him to be doing any of the theatre work on me so I was a bit surprised when the nurses told me who would be doing it. Then it was a bit of a rush to get changed etc. as he was waiting for me, or should I say an orderly named Graeme who I was to discover only got his trolley-bed licence out of a packet of cornflakes that morning!

I got to see the Professor before I went to sleep and I thought to myself jokingly well now we've seen each other when we're both looking our worst. But seriously, after I had thought that I said I should be putting a tent out in the passageway because I was only here on 11th October and it was now only the 15h November, and he told me that I would be back in two weeks time. I couldn't believe my ears as I didn't have any period and I thought that you always had to have one before egg retrieval. I pointed to my stomach and said that's impossible as there's nothing—meaning no period. I know that he knew what I was talking about because he said he would come and see me after I had my sleep. I said how embarrassing it was to be there so often and he just simply said that he would put a plaque on the wall saying "Debbie has been here often".

After having my normal amount of needles (this time the dose was 450 units, the highest you can go) I had the usual blood tests and scans which showed that everything was going nicely for once. So well in fact, that one of the nurses actually shook my hand! The original plan was for me to do an antagonist cycle, which meant to stop any ovulation which results through the progesterone being too high. When it came to starting the drug it was discovered that there wasn't any as the amount they had in storage was out of date, so I had to continue using the nasal spray—Syneral.

On the tenth day of the cycle, I nearly had heart failure as the nasal spray ran out and this occurred after they had checked the bottle and said there would be enough. I phoned the clinic and advised them of my problem, expecting them to say that I would need to buy another bottle, but they said it didn't matter as the drug stays in your system for up to two weeks. What a relief!

Finally it was time for the egg pick up. The professor was going to do it but he had an emergency to attend to which was very understandable after my glowing performances! I had the same doctor that had drained the cyst in October, better than another strange doctor I thought. As I had expected at least five eggs (going by what was on the scans) I was in for a major shock when I first woke up because there was no number written on the back of my hand. Seeing as they normally write the number there, I immediately assumed there were no eggs and my heart just sank. The male nurse who was looking after me in recovery must have noticed the expression on my face and he said "you're not smiling?" All I could think of was what had I done all this for, for nothing.

When one of the clinic nurses came to visit all of the people who had had egg collection, I was very relieved when I was given my piece of paper stating that they had gotten four eggs and my spirits picked up a lot. The next day I rang up to find out how many eggs had actually been fertilised only to be told a very disappointing one. By now I was in a negative frame of mind, thinking it would be a miracle, if in fact the embryo was still alive on Monday. It was transferred by the professor himself who was being very fussy to the point of even turning the air-conditioning off. I was quite disappointed with the fact that the embryo only rated a 3 whereas the last one I had rated as perfect. I commented to the nurse my surprise the embryo was still alive and she asked why, so I told her how there was no number written on my hand on Friday and she must have gone and told the professor because when he saw me he asked me whether there was number written on your hand and I said no, and I got the feeling that he wasn't impressed, so I wondered whether he said anything to the doctor concerned.

The hardest thing for me to cope with in regard to being a patient of the professor is the level of his sincerity in wanting to help me. I knew he really wanted it to work because he said as he was leaving "good luck with the little guy" which meant a lot to me as I already had a feeling that the embryo wasn't going to make it. That was the most likely due to all of the back luck I had had in the past, after all, it was the last chance for me to have a child which was genetically linked to me. I was feeling it very keenly as I didn't have any emotional connection with my birth mother and now this was my last chance to have a child with my own bloodline.

I had a blood sample taken the same day to make sure the hormone as going up and guess what? It was 283 which I thought was really good as it was ten points higher than the same time at my last attempt. I had started using the progesterone help and now all I could do was hope for a miracle. It wasn't long before I started feeling very ill, as in 'sick as a dog' and no wonder—the blood test which was done on the Friday showed the level was now up to 600. I could hardly believe my ears when they told me and I thought they might have made a mistake. I was meant to have my second needle of 1000 units of Pregnyl, but they advised me not to have it until the Monday and then only a half dose. This really started to worry me because the order had been given by none other than the doctor who I had dumped for the professor. Well, by Sunday I had the horrible feeling that things were on a downward slope because I started to feel a bit different, and this to me was not a good sign. I was on my way back home when I got this strange sensation all around my uterus, the best way I could describe it was like when you're going to start a period. Part of me knew I was in trouble, but yet another part of me was holding on to a glimmer of hope that the poor little thing—the embryo, would somehow survive.

As you can probably guess, my gut feeling was right yet again, much to my horror. I did have the needle on the Monday as requested and I also sent a blood sample down to the clinic, but the result was very, very bad as the progesterone had dropped now to a mere 73. This nearly broke my heart as I thought to myself, how on earth could it (the embryo), be doing so well and then look as if it was going to die. I honestly believe the pregnancy lasted for one whole week that time, which doesn't sound like very long to most people, but to me it was a major achievement. I rang the clinic on 17th December as requested to find out the results of the blood sample taken the day before, to check it if was bad or good news. As you can guess, the result wasn't what I wanted to hear, the progesterone had dropped to 13. It was totally beyond me how on earth it could have been going so well, only to end up like this again.

I must have had rocks in my head because I when I took a shower, I talked to it and pleaded with it to keep going if it could, because it was really wanted.

I got my period on 17th as expected, but nothing had prepared me for what was about to happen. I had expected a fairly normal period to occur, but I was in for a major shock. When I lost the last embryo, there was only a piece of transparent stretchy skin and an abnormal clot and the normal abdominal pains before the infection set in. On the 18th I had gone to work as normal, because as I said, I had no warning that on that morning I was going to get into trouble with a capital 'T'. Apart from feeling sad which I can normally cover up, I wasn't feeling too bad physically, but by 11. 30am that had all changed.

I went to the toilet and we all do, only to find that I had passed something which is difficult to describe. To me it reinforced what I had thought earlier and that was I felt the embryo had lived for at least a week. It's best described as being a piece of human tissue which was very crimson red in colour, but the length of it is what completely threw me emotionally, it was not quite as long as about half the length of the tampon it came out on, and it looked as if it was folded over like a cocoon. I wanted to, but I couldn't touch it because I didn't know if it contained the dead embryo. My friend was out and I had to try and find her or her mother via her mobile phone because I knew I had to get to the clinic within a short time to give it to them to send away, otherwise I ran the risk of not being believed by the clinic. Fortunately I used my brain or what was left of it and realised that I needed to wrap it in cling wrap to stop it from drying out. The phone call to my friend's mother was the hardest phone call that I have ever had to make, I just said to her that if she could please find her daughter and send her home because I thought I had just lost the embryo. By the time my friend got home it was just about more than I could handle, I wasn't feeling too good and by the time I arrived at the medical centre, I didn't care which doctor I was seen by, as long as it was someone who would believe me. Even though it only took about ten minutes to drive to the clinic, it seemed to take forever. Here was I with a possible embryo wrapped in cling wrap, sitting in the console of our car. I don't think anyone would expect the hopes of parenthood to end like that.

They were really good to me at the clinic, apart from the fact that I had to try and explain it all again to a new lady doctor, which was in my favour a bit because she was very kind and compassionate. I couldn't help but cry a little bit as I hadn't expected to see what I saw and on top of it all, I was now having the most cruel muscle spasms that I had ever had in my life. They were even reaching up under my rib cage to a point where it affected the way I was breathing. They arranged for me to go to Berri for a scan to see if all the embryo material had been expelled or not, so I drove home to try and find Ian at work to get him to take me up to the appointment, because I was in no shape to drive myself by that stage, with the constant pain especially on the right side of my abdomen. I was thinking to myself, not this side again as that is what had to be fixed up last time. When Ian got home I was quite disappointed by his first response, he just looked at me and said "you didn't give me much warning", and I thought boy, oh boy. I never had any warning at all! What also upset me was the fact that he should have been able to tell by the look on my face that something was very wrong, and this was only the second time in eight years that I had called him home from work. When we were ready to leave for Berri, I had to go to the toilet again and found that I had passed the biggest clot that I had ever seen, so I got Ian to drop it off at the surgery again so they could send it away with the first sample.

The trip to Berri was dreadful as I couldn't wear my seatbelt and Ian could have driven a lot faster, more than 110kph, I said to him that we had a piece of paper stating that I had a severe medical problem and I was quite sure that we would get out of any speeding ticket if we were stopped. I had been told to try and drink a litre of water which was very difficult because it was just over an hour until the scan and my stomach was so sore and the pain very constant. I hadn't been given any painkillers because the doctor wasn't sure what she would have to do for me until she knew the results of the scan. We didn't have to wait that long really, but still, it felt like ages to me because I was bent over to try and help me cope with the pain. After I was finished with, I asked for the scan pictures as I usually did, but they told me that they wouldn't know the results until tomorrow because there was no doctor there to check the scan pictures. Things then got a little worse. The whole time Ian had been waiting for me, he was reading a book and then decided he would like to get some lunch. Again, I had to wait for ten minutes while they were making his lunch and this really cheesed me off because he knew that we had to get back to the local Medical Clinic to find out what we had to do next. When we told the doctor that we had no results with us, she had to convince the person who did the scan that she really needed to know the results because of my situation. The poor doctor spent ages trying to get in contact with the clinic to tell them the bad news, only to find that they were between buildings and having trouble with the phone lines. I thought to myself—here we go again! Last time I ended up in a mess they couldn't be contacted either. I explained that last time things had been bad and I ended up with a severe infection and had to be sent to Adelaide by plane, so I was given antibiotics just in case. Ian really peeved me off because he said that I was complaining, and I thought to myself I'm going through emotional hell and you say I'm complaining? I had to take the pills twice a day for five days.

To my horror, Ian went out that night, leaving me home alone because it seems he didn't have the sense or brains to phone his friend and explain that he should stay home with his wife in light of what had happened that day. He had been taking children on horse rides for Christmas in the evenings and instead of realising that it was not appropriate at this point, he felt that he might as well be helping out the community because I wasn't talking to him. The fact was that I was totally spun out mentally so that I wasn't aware of what was going on around me. I just sat on the front verandah and wondered just how much worse things could get. It was not only a week before Christmas Day and two weeks before I had been hoping for a Christmas miracle, but it had all gone dreadfully wrong. On the Thursday I ended up going back to see the doctor again because I was still having the major muscle spasms and I simply didn't understand the reason why. I found out that the human tissue that I had passed had come through a very closed cervix so I started to gain some understanding of the reason why I was in such a physical mess.

I was given more pills to take as by now the doctor had been able to talk to Cathy, one of the nurses at Repromed, the pills were actually special pain killers for severe uterine spasms and had to be taken two, three times per day or as needed. By now I also had noticed that my urine was only just coming out in a very slow dribble, which didn't surprise me considering the condition that I was in, and I thought it was just a matter of time and it would correct itself. The bleeding kept going for four days and then stopped. I thought that was a bit unusual, but I wasn't to know any different. During my second visit on the Wednesday, the doctor was trying to involve Ian and just asked how he was feeling, because after all it was his or should I say—our baby or embryo that had lost, and his reply was quite rude. He just said to her "you wouldn't like to know what I think". As if I wasn't going through enough! I just covered for him and said that he didn't like technology, so hopefully it didn't make her feel that Ian was being rude to her.

Four days after the first bleeding had stopped, it restarted, only this time it was bright red and it also had to be continually wiped out of my vagina because it wasn't flowing properly. This continued for ten days, which to me was very distressing. Now I was just hoping that the reproductive specialists were prepared to believe what the doctors were saying because I felt that I wouldn't get very far if they didn't.

On the Friday or Saturday, my brother phoned to let me know that I had a new little niece and as much as I was happy for him, I thought, how strange that life can get, in that we had lost an embryo and gained a niece in a very short space of time. Peter was quite sympathetic towards me and told me to look after myself. I really appreciated his comments as it wasn't something I heard much from Ian.

Ian started to appear very uncaring, doing stupid things like watching cartoons without thinking that maybe it was upsetting to me in the current circumstances. After all, there were no small children of our own to sit and watch them with him. By Saturday morning it was all too much for me and I ended up screaming at him because he had no idea of the emotional pain that it was causing. All I wanted was for him to give me a hug and hold me, but it never happened. The only time he was interested in giving me a hug was when his hormones went through the roof and when I refused, what a protest! I started to think that maybe I had married an animal, but then sometimes animals are capable of showing more compassion than I had been shown. I really felt it was sad because how could a person live for nearly forty years and not have any idea of what compassion was or when it was needed.

I tried to explain it to him and it was quite evident that he had limited comprehension on the subject. His sister rang and I made sure she knew, just in case Ian hadn't told her because after all, she had the right to know and she was quite nice about it and just said "bugger", but in a nice way. My mum also happened to ring up but I didn't have much to say as not much had been happening. I hadn't told her about the last IVF attempt. She said "I hope you're not still trying for a baby?" I couldn't believe what I had heard. How could someone say something like that and as for the timing, well it couldn't have been worse.

On the Monday I went and looked after the kids as normal and I didn't mind it. I got to give them hugs which I found to be like therapy. Ian and I were invited to go to my friend's sister's place for Christmas morning, to see the children open their presents. We went along and I felt that at least they cared enough that they didn't want us to be left alone at Christmas. Ian wasn't keen on the idea, but as I said to him—at least we were being thought of which meant a lot to me. What really surprised me was the fact that my friend's whole family had all contributed towards a gift voucher for me for Christmas and every time I see them now, I think to myself you didn't have to do that for me. I don't think they will ever know just how much it meant to me at the time.

On the 21st January, 2003, I ended up going to the doctor again because I was still getting muscle spasms and also frequent urination, sometimes up to twelve times in twenty four hours, and in pathetic amounts as low as 55mls. I thought that maybe I had an infection again because I had had one on the 2nd December. I also went to have some scans done to try and see what was going on, or at least eliminate some possibilities. The scans were actually quite painful which certainly wasn't normal for me, so I was quite sure something wasn't right. I just hoped that the problem could be sorted out really soon because I had been like it for nearly two months. I was given more antibiotics just in case, but it didn't change anything so I was off to the doctors again on 12th February, only to be put back on pills that were meant to relax my bladder muscles so I didn't have to go to the toilet so often. So much for those pills, what a total waste of time as the only thing they managed to do was to dry out my mouth so I was off to see a urologist (plumbing department). Logic told me that after two months it should have righted itself if it was going to. I only had to wait two weeks to get in because I was willing to travel to Adelaide instead of waiting for another month. The specialist was quite good and arranged for me to have day surgery at our local hospital which was really great as I didn't have to go back to the city and rely on others.

Until now, mum didn't know anything at all and I was planning for it to stay that way because of past experience with her on this matter. I only had to wait another two weeks before my surgery date and while I was waiting, I was given more pills to try, which were even stronger. The side effects made them not worth taking, my mouth was like chalk and mentally I felt like I was loopy. I felt dopey all the time so I only took them for a week because they made no difference to the real problem. I was last on the list for the surgical patients and I didn't get to have my go until midday, and of course, my veins were totally shut down to the point that when the anaesthetist tried to put the needle in so he could knock me out, I didn't even bleed, so out came the gas which didn't surprise me in the least.

The whole idea of this surgery was to inspect the inside of my bladder to make sure that there was nothing on the inside contributing to the problems I was having, so the doctor also filled my bladder to make sure it could expand properly. When I woke up I felt a bit sore, and then I noticed that I was on a saline drip. I guess I must have been pretty dehydrated and when I was in the second stage recovery room, I was the only person with a drip in. The specialist saw me before I left the hospital and he told me that everything looked alright on the inside and that my bladder held more than I said. I didn't appreciate that comment because the only thing I was asked to write down was how much I had been drinking, when and how often I was passing urine and when I went to the toilet. I honestly believe it was something to do with the muscles because as I said before, I never had spasms like that before, in my entire life. I needed to go back in early May, which was good because by then I would have seen my favourite professor, so I could only hope that he would have some idea of what was going on and be able to rectify it somehow.

Unbeknown to me, Ian had arranged for his two nephews to come and stay with us in the middle of February because they were having trouble getting work where they lived. I was in total shock because how on earth did he make this decision without even talking to me. Surely I was entitled to have some say in the matter as his wife. The first thing I knew was when I got a call to say they were on their way. I will never understand why on earth their mother didn't have the sense to talk to me personally, to see if I was feeling up to it because it was less than two months since I had miscarried. I knew for a fact that I certainly wasn't ready for anything like this. Besides trying to cope with the remaining physical trauma of the miscarriage, I was struggling emotionally trying to handle what had happened. I was now struggling to cope with the reality of never being able to have a biological child of my own. I came to the realisation that people don't think of anyone but themselves, which I felt was really sad because those people miss out on a lot when you think about it.

I could never in a lifetime have guessed what type of people were coming to live in our home. Most of the time I was so close to tears, it was just beyond a joke. I was brought up to be respectful to the older generation and yet Ian was allowing his nephews to treat me—his wife, like dirt, and when I made the very strong suggestion that they should leave our home he tried to tell me that I would have to leave if I pushed it any further. I quickly had to develop a survival strategy which included going out most nights. I was totally sick of them being in our home all the time but I couldn't get it through Ian's thick head that we, as a married couple, need time together alone. I told him that our marriage was far more important than his nephews. As you can imagine, this didn't go down too well with Ian but I felt that I had no choice but to fight for what I truly believed in—my marriage. I had no idea just how Ian thought I would accept their disgraceful behaviour. They weren't even capable of setting the dinner table without being stupid, let alone respecting my standards of conduct in our home. All I can say, out of politeness, is that if I had treated any of my aunts or uncles the same way Ian's nephews treated me, I would have had such a sore backside I wouldn't have been able to sit down for a week. To make matters even worse, Ian let them get away with their rotten behaviour and in no way did he stick up for me as his wife, which made me feel like a piece of junk. I almost walked out on more than one occasion.

Well, on 19th March, I decided that I would go and have another talk with one of the local doctors. On the weekend I had noticed something different with regard to my pain problem. I started to believe that maybe my cervix might have something to do with it because Ian and I had been having 'fun'. Sadly, I spent the rest of the day wondering if it had been worth it or not (just kidding). I had made it clear that I wasn't prepared to take the pills to relax the muscles all the time, because they weren't fixing the problem and the doctor agreed. He thought I may have some scar tissue near my bladder and uterus which seemed to make sense as it felt like something was pulling. I made a little joke about the professor being able to write a new book called 'Professional Disasters' and I could be in it, and the doctor said "do you think you could be chapter one?"

I now only had to wait until the following Wednesday to see the professor and I had very mixed feelings. I felt quite sad because this same man had wished me luck when the last embryo was transferred and cared enough to get the counsellor to phone me at home when things went wrong, to make sure that I was alright. I really didn't understand society anymore because the response I got from the people who should have known better, was totally appalling compared with how I was being treated by some of the people at the clinic.

Ian's parents came to visit for a week in March and stayed at the caravan park which suited me just fine. The two nephews were still living with us and there was simply no more room for anyone else. The week went quite well and we seemed to enjoy each others company. I very carefully broached the subject with his mother about my miscarriage, only to find out that she had been told by my sister-in-law before Christmas. She couldn't even be bothered to say hello to me, let alone see if I was alright. As for my own mum, she didn't know I was trying again. She just happened to phone before Christmas and said again "I hope you're not still trying for a baby". I couldn't believe the timing so I just made out that there was nothing wrong, after all, she was 80 years of age.

I made a decision to try and have a family with donated embryos, and I decided to discuss this with my mother-in-law, thinking that surely she would show some interest, but how wrong I was. I explained to her that we had been told about the background of the donating parents including their physical description, so we would have some idea of what we would be getting, if we were by some miracle successful. I then went on to explain that we would be willing to let the child meet the biological parents if everyone agreed. My, oh my! I wasn't prepared for what she said next, she told me it wasn't necessary, as long as we knew any medical information that was deemed important. I found this very, very hard to digest because in my mind, when you have been given a priceless gift such as a child, how on earth could you have such a selfish attitude, and besides from where I had been in my life, I personally felt that I wouldn't have the right to deny the child contact with its biological family. I also explained that the hardest part of the whole situation was there wouldn't be any genetic continuity. The next comment from my mother-in-law was the bone chilling statement that I was "just making a big issue out of it". I couldn't believe my ears. How could this woman not show or feel any compassion, considering the circumstances. I didn't say that because I felt she would think I was whinging, but it was a fact and I found it quite sad because there would be three generations of non-biological relatives in one family.

At last, 26th March arrived and I was having very mixed feelings to say the least. I had booked out of the motel after Ian and the boys had left to go to Magic Mountain for the day. The clinic had since settled into their new building, so I didn't have to go to the hospital. This was a lot better as I didn't have to travel to the other side of the city. As for the new building, it was very nice to say the least, with a lovely new smell. I didn't have to wait long before it was my appointment time. The professor was very nice to me and asked if I was finding it hard, and I explained that if I didn't have the stomach pains, I probably wouldn't get so upset all the time, but then again I didn't feel shame in the fact that I cried a bit because to me it was a very lonely experience and no matter how kind people were to me, nothing seemed to be able to stop the feelings of isolation. I also told him what happened the day I lost the embryo so he would be able to get some understanding of what may have gone wrong.

The events of that day that I officially miscarried will be forever imprinted on my memory because it was nothing short of a tragedy as far as I was concerned. The result of my visit to the professor was excellent, he acknowledged that I HAD been pregnant, but he didn't understand why the pain had been so severe because he would have expected that sort of thing to happen later in the pregnancy. He answered all of my many questions and I was quite pleased with the replies. I had also had six tubes of blood taken to test for up to nine different things and the good part was that they could help me with any problems which may have shown up as a result. At least it would show up any unknown conditions that I may have had. We found out that we were eligible for donated embryos.

It was a big thing to emotionally to give up one's genetics, but I had come to the conclusion that it might be my own eggs that were the problem because I had never had any major success in getting a lot of eggs at retrieval time. I decided that I would most likely have better luck with donated embryos because they were donated by couples who had been successful, so they definitely worked. I don't think anyone could really understand what this decision was costing me emotionally because I never had my own biological mother, and now I could never have my own biological children either. One sad thing about this was there would always be a lot of questions about myself as a toddler which could never be answered. This wouldn't have been so much of a problem if we had at least been able to conceive through sperm donation alone. At the same time though, I could see the good side of our decision and that was that it was fairer on Ian if there was no genetic link to me either, so then we were both equal.

In October 2003 I paid the $2000 work up fee. We had to pay this to be put on the waiting list and it also covered the donating couples' blood test expenses. The nurse that would be looking after us sent us some forms to fill in so they could match us to any embryos which became available. I was actually quite excited because I believed that maybe, just maybe, we had a better chance of becoming parents. We had three chances with embryos as they became available. Now we just had to wait and I didn't mind because the clinic didn't get a lot of embryo donations.

I now decided that I would write to the cemetery committee because I felt that I had an idea that would be good for the community. My idea, I explained, was that I would like to see a plaque of some sort, put up in memory of the babies who didn't have graves for their parents to visit. I wanted the plaque to be for parents who had lost babies through miscarriage and premature births. In South Australia, if a child was born before seventeen or 18 weeks gestation it wasn't compulsory by law for the child to be buried in the cemetery. In other words, the hospital would dispose of the foetus. I was very pleased with the outcome of my letter, because at no cost to me, a lovely plaque was placed on the wishing well, complete with swinging bucket and facing west which I felt was quite poignant.

The poem on the plaque reads as follows:

Dedicated to all those babies who have been lost before they were born but are still loved and missed.

How do we get to say goodbye when you never arrived? You sent a message to our hearts to tell us you were on your way but before we had a chance to hold you our time together had passed and you our precious had gone to be a bright shining star.

Sometimes I just stand and look at the well and watch the empty bucket swing in the wind and wonder what our children would have been like, and at the same time I feel totally empty inside. I truly feel that the people who have families have no idea of what goes on in the minds of those who have no family because there are so many milestones in life that a childless couple never get to celebrate.

That month surprise, surprise, the South Australian State Government opened Pandora's box by announcing that they had extended the time frame in which prosecution could take place against people who had sexually abused children (former state wards) in their care. To be a Ward of the State, you had to be under the guardianship of the Minister until you turned eighteen. A hotline was set up so those who knew, or felt that had been affected by this horrific problem, could call and speak to a police officer.

I knew that I had a problem in this area as I had memories that were no good and also the way I reacted on my honeymoon was certainly not normal. I had to convince myself that it couldn't be my imagination after ten years. Finally, after two weeks of thinking whether I did or didn't, I picked up the phone and called. I was given a reference number. A policeman did call back, and I couldn't believe how it ended. I told him honestly what I could remember and the circumstances at the time and he suggested that maybe I had overreacted to a smack on the backside because he couldn't find any hard evidence in my welfare files, and that maybe I should try some counselling to try and sort out what may have caused my problems.

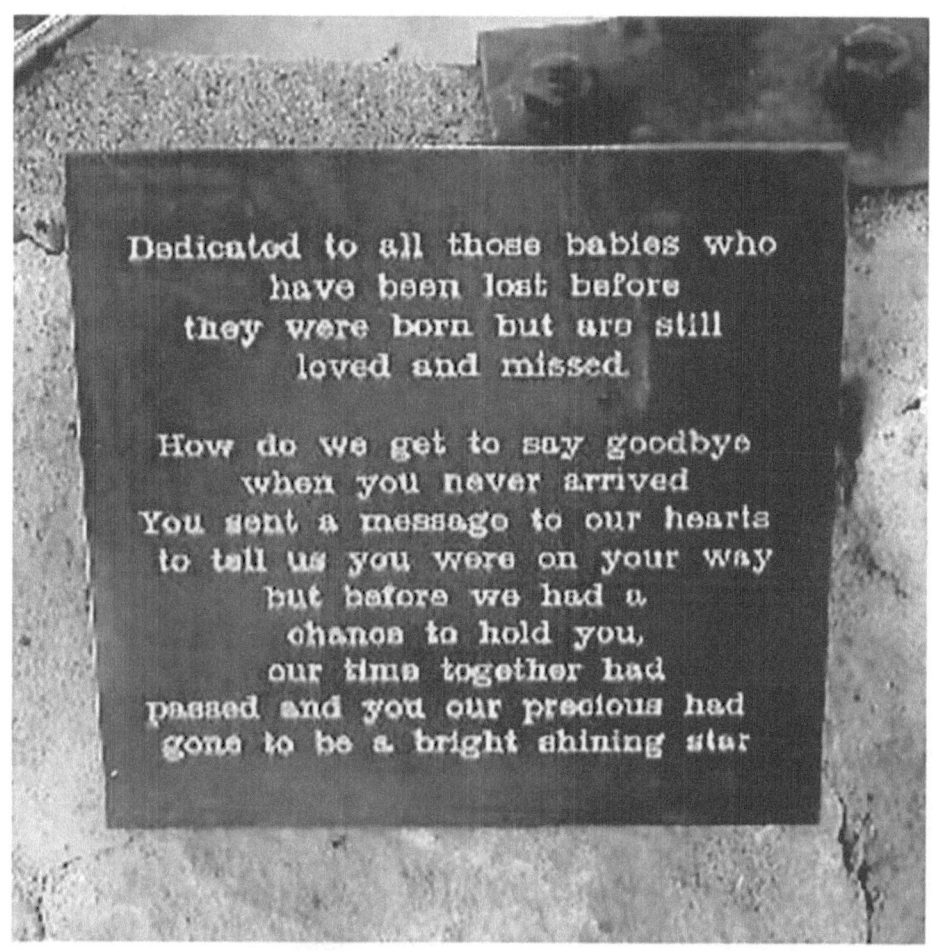

Dedicated to all those babies who
have been lost before
they were born but are still
loved and missed.

How do we get to say goodbye
when you never arrived
You sent a message to our hearts
to tell us you were on your way
but before we had a
chance to hold you,
our time together had
passed and you our precious had
gone to be a bright shining star

After that, I thought why on earth I bothered if that's how they were going to treat me. In early March I did start some counselling sessions through the local Health Service. After a couple of visits, I had to change counsellors as my first one was taking time off and I ended up with a Scotsman. I was finding it very beneficial, even though Ian sadly wasn't interested in coming, even just to find out how the brain works, which I think would have made things a lot easier at home for me. Our nocturnal activities went down a slippery slope as a result of his rotten lazy attitude because I decided that he wasn't prepared to be thoughtful to say the least, I wasn't going to advertise any interest that I may have felt. Why should I put up with things that I couldn't handle? It was now time to put on paper my trigger points (the things that I felt I couldn't handle being done to me). This was very, very hard for me to do as it made me feel totally horrible emotionally, plus it was very draining. When I showed the counsellor and explained it, he went very quiet and became very concerned. He rang up the police department to get their opinion, and their spin on it was that I could have been sexually abused. It was pointed out to me that our brain has a Mental Memory and also a Physical Memory. Which makes a lot of sense when you think of how I react in different situations, because the trigger points don't register unless touched in the same way (although not intentionally) by others. I thought to myself—great. Well it was an improvement on the reaction from the last policeman I spoke to. It was suggested to me that I could, if I want to, talk to a policewoman in the local area, but by the same token she had already stated that she would not do anything with regard to my complaint. As far as I could see it would have been a waste of my time and emotional energy. I didn't understand why she was like that because she was fully aware of the changes in the law and besides, didn't she have any idea of how much it takes out of you to discuss such a personal matter?

The counselling sessions were going well until I was advised that my second counsellor in as many months was losing his position in the Health Service, due to cutbacks. I couldn't believe my luck, or should I say—lack of it.

I had a choice to make, to try and paddle my own canoe at home or I could write to one of the politicians to see if there was any funding available for people in my position because I knew one thing for sure, and that was that I shouldn't have to pay for the counselling sessions because the problem was not my fault as I was a State Ward. I did, after some time, get a reply offering me free counselling which was being coordinated by Relationships Australia, so off I went to my first session. I didn't take too long in the interview for me to realise that this wasn't going to work because there's nothing worse than after every sentence you say, the person listening to you uses the word yeah! How on earth was I supposed to open up to this lady when I kept losing my train of thought before I could get it out because of her bad speech habits?

Finally I got consent to see someone else and that turned out well. Only at these counselling sessions did I realise what sort of emotional mess I was in.

On 15th December, 2004 I travelled to Adelaide to speak to one of the officials who was helping at the Mullighan Inquiry which had been launched on the 8th. I found the process of trying to explain myself to a total stranger very isolating as I had to do my best to tell my story so the Commission could grasp the extent of my personal problems. Fortunately I had kept most of my official paperwork from the welfare which I had collected over the years, so it was a lot easier in that regard.

In July 2004 we received a letter from the clinic with regard to an appointment with another professor who specialised in patients who had problems with pregnancy. Surprise, surprise! I should have seen him a lot earlier than this. He was very nice to both of us and I had to have another lot of blood tests done to double check things to give us the best chance of things going in the right direction for us at last. I simply could not believe the difference in attitude between the two professors and the rest of the circus. The reason why I use the word circus is because I honestly believe that the majority were only pretending to have an interest in reproductive medicine. By their actions (or lack of action I should say), it showed that their heart wasn't in their work ethic and I couldn't let myself even begin to imagine how many couples had gone without children because of this problem. These types of doctors do not have the right to work in a world class facility. The new professor started me on vitamin pills because he felt I needed them after he saw my blood test results. In one sense I was happy to be taking them (for obvious reasons), but on the other hand, I was angry that nobody had bothered to check whether or not I needed them for my own embryos, but I was automatically given them when I had given up on my own genetics. To me that was an example of having two standards of treatment which was totally unethical. In the middle of 2004, a group of embryos became available, and we accepted them, but we didn't have them transferred because by now we had made big plans to go to America for three weeks in October. I knew it would be totally stupid in my situation to attempt a pregnancy before going away because knowing my luck, if the pregnancy did work, I would most likely get into bother while I was overseas.

Part of the reason for going so far away for our holiday was to get Ian away from everyone, and I mean everyone he knew, so we could rediscover each other and give me a chance to see if he was still the same person I had married. We flew out of Melbourne at 10am and by 3pm it was getting dark as we were entering the northern hemisphere. It was really weird trying to make believe it was night time when really in our mentality, it was still afternoon. To pass the time I tried to become an expert on playing hangman with my in flight computer, which was very time consuming. After all, I had nowhere to go!

We arrived in Los Angeles at 7am and it was a real eye opener. We had never been to such a busy airport so early in the day. By the time we had gone through customs, it was time to start our last routine again, this time catching a domestic flight to New York. This trip took about five hours and only then did I fully realise just how wide the land we were crossing was. We arrived after sunset and we had the taxi ride of a lifetime, with Ian hanging on for dear life. He'd never been with a taxi driver who drove the way this one did. Personally I thought it was so funny because this bloke was like a comedian.

After settling in to our hotel on 7th Avenue, we had a look around outside and to our amazement the human traffic just kept on moving. We spent a lot of time in Times Square where the electronic screens are never the same for very long. My favourite eating place was just up the street from our hotel, it was called Fluffy's café and they had so many different types of treats that I had grown used to when I lived in North America. Our time in this great city was totally amazing and we accomplished quite a lot I thought. The tourist lines taught us a lot of patience and you learn a lot while you're waiting around, talking to other tourists while the lines are on the move. It took us four hours to finally arrive at the Statue of Liberty which, by the way, is truly amazing and I could have quite easily spent a lot longer with her on her beautifully landscaped island.

Along with the rest of the tourists, we were drawn to the Empire State Building after we had our tea. That queue was just as long if not longer, and it still took three hours to just get to the lift to go up to the 80th floor, but I can't stress enough that it was well worth the wait and the gift shop was one of the biggest gift shops that I have seen in a very long time. We went on a helicopter ride which was great and we flew over most of the major landmarks which certainly gave us a different angle on things. It was now time to leave the Big Apple as they call it, so Ian and I caught an Amtrak train down to Orlando, a trip which took twenty four hours. I didn't mind as it gave us time to unwind before we arrived. North America had some spectacular scenery on the eastside. Our night meal was excellent and the waiter, who was from Chile, was great and once he knew where we were from, the first topic of discussion was beer! He wanted to know what types of beer we had. Poor Ian couldn't understand his accent so I ended up having to repeat most of the conversation. In between going to Disney Parks, we did as much or as little as we wanted, which mostly involved spending time around the pool talking to people from many nations who were convinced that Florida was holiday central, and we could see why. This was the quickest ten days of my life. Soon it was time to pack our bags again to spend five days in Venice Beach. When we arrived at the Orlando Airport I couldn't believe the level of security, it was as if they were all paranoid, standing around waiting for something to happen. The thing that annoyed me most was the fact that we even had to take our shoes and socks off. As if someone was going to put some type of device in between their toes!

To me the saddest part of the whole terrorist alert issue is that I truly feel people have forgotten that 98% of the world's population are decent living people who are simply minding their own business.

Our last holiday stop was at Venice Beach in Los Angeles, which in many ways lost its appeal for me before we had even discovered it. It seemed that there were two different types of crowds, one on the weekend and the other midweek which by the look of things consisted mostly of the unemployed. Ian and I did a lot of walking around the main city centre of Los Angeles in a downpour of rain. Ian said once we were wet, why worry, but we did manage to stumble across the city library which had eight floors. We had never seen so many books before, in one place. We did a morning VIP tour of Hollywood which was an eye-opener because when you saw it on television, it didn't look the same. I would have like to have some more time to check out Rodeo Drive where all the expensive shops were. When it was lunchtime, we were shown where to get really great food and all was going just fine until the bus went over a speed bump and as luck would have it, we had bought thick shakes. How embarrassing! Here I was sitting in the bus in the front row, with chocolate thick shake between my legs, and creating a lovely circular brown patch on my white t-shirt. Much to my horror Ian said aloud so all could hear "Deb, I can't take you anywhere!" I just wished that I could have disappeared. It didn't take too long to see the funny side of the whole episode though as we were on our way to Universal Studios for what turned out to be a fun time, even though I had been on all the rides when I lived with my first family.

Now it was time to rejoin the real world and go back to the old routine. Like they say, all good things must come to an end. The trip back across the Pacific was good. We didn't leave until midnight, arriving back in Melbourne around 7am. We managed to get some sleep in between talking with a group of pensioners who were on a whirlwind trip of Australia and New Zealand. We came to the conclusion that most foreigners have no idea of just how big Australia is. I had to laugh when we cleared customs and someone in the group made the comment that they had nobody to meet them so Ian went around hugging the ladies saying "welcome to Australia." Sometimes things seem so funny when you're tired. We had to catch another flight to Adelaide and we were sitting in the waiting lounge and another group of ladies were bragging about just how well they had managed to get out of bed on time. couldn't help but think to myself, ladies, if you only knew what I had been up to this morning, as I had been watching the sun since 3am while they were still sleeping.

I felt so good physically after my time away that I decided I should have a break every eighteen months to two years. You don't get any medals for wearing yourself out.

I decided that we should have the first of the embryos transferred when the clinic opened after the Christmas break because I didn't want to have a bummer of a Christmas day. Well, as for the transfer cycle itself, it went really well and I was feeling positive, even though only one out of the batch of 4 had survived the thawing process. The quality of the embryo was excellent which made me think that my chances would be quite good. I was going to use the three progesterone pessaries a day, one every 8 hours. In some ways it was like a religious ritual, I couldn't be a minute late. Sadly things went great until day five after the transfer when I was walking down the street and I felt what could only be described as a sharp pain in my uterine area and I immediately thought oh no, not again! I had learnt from past experience, the difference between when the embryo was living and when things had gone wrong. It was at this point that I was starting to ask myself how on earth I could be such a defective female. I wasn't even capable of keeping a poor little embryo going for two full weeks. As we had three goes at this program, and even though I felt it badly, I wasn't too worried because we still had two more tries left before we were out the back door as far as the clinic was concerned.

The timing of this failure to get pregnant yet again could not have come at a worse time because on the 15th March, 2005 I had to meet the Commissioner, Mr Mullighan. This meeting was just a week after finding out that we had been unsuccessful, so I was feeling bad enough to start with. The Commission had provided accommodation and meals and I only had to walk over the street, which in itself seemed to take forever as I never in a lifetime imagined that after thirty odd years, my time in the welfare department would become an open book and all of my inner most emotions and feelings would surface.

Mr Mullighan was really kind to me and he did his best to discuss this very sensitive issue in the gentlest manner possible. Whoever chose Mr Mullighan for this horrific job could not have made a better choice. I felt sorry for him, having to ask people very personal questions about a really sensitive issue. In some ways I didn't feel as if I had been much help to him. Part of the problem was that at the time when things went really wrong for me, I was less than six years old and being given tranquilisers of some sort, so that meant that some of memories were foggy. When I said to him that I didn't know if what I had told him was of much help, he assured me that it was and I had to keep reminding myself that I was very young at that time and I couldn't be expected to remember any better than I had. Even though at the meeting I managed to hold myself together emotionally, it did take an awful lot out of me and I felt physically drained as well, to the point that even when I had been home for two days, I just didn't know what to do with myself and I just walked around the house like a lost soul. The saddest part of the whole problem was that the people who committed these crimes against children, forgot one very, very important thing, and that is the fact that they had been entrusted to look after other peoples children. Ian wasn't much help because he said I had been acting weird since I got home and asked me what was wrong. I said OK, I'm not coping well with what I had been through and a hug would be good, but no surprise—it just fell on deaf ears. For a while I felt very alone. I hadn't even told Mum what was going on because I didn't want to hear any horrible remarks.

When I received my copy of the transcript, I went through it once and since then I haven't looked at again. It made me feel so dreadful inside because it was beyond me how I managed to get myself into those predicaments.

My next attempt at getting pregnant ended up the same except this time things didn't go wrong until day nine after the transfer, which in some ways was encouraging despite yet another round of disappointment. This time the alarm bells went off, but I was doing everything in my power to keep things going. These last two attempts I didn't blame anyone because after all, everything that could be done was being done so it was nobody's fault. I wrote to the professor requesting that a small camera be used to check my uterus, just in case there was anything that could be causing this problem. I thought in fairness to myself, I should find out if I wasn't going to be able to hold the embryos because then it would be pointless having any more tries, plus the embryos could be donated to another couple. Well, I was in for a shock. This test should have been done two years earlier when I had the last laparoscopy at the hospital in Adelaide. The professor told me that he had ordered it to be done, but I was never told. Fortunately I had kept my discharge papers which proved my point, so off to hospital I had to go—again. By this stage I was really livid because I thought to myself, pity help them if they find something which could and should have been detected before we started the current program. This operation was done by the same doctor who had been ordered to do it two years before so I was far from happy as I felt that he was totally incompetent. I had come to the strong conclusion that some doctors should not be doctors because what happened just before the operation was remarkable to say the least. I couldn't believe just how thick the assistant doctor was. I was asked to provide a urine sample to prove that I wasn't pregnant. I went on to tell him that I couldn't be for two reasons; because my husband had no sperm and most importantly, I was on day 10 of my current cycle and as far as I could work out, those two factors didn't allow for pregnancy. I don't know just how I managed to hold my tongue but this jerk went on to insist that I do the test anyway. This bum might as well put a knife through my heart and put me out of my misery. I was now at the stage of wondering just how much more rubbish I could handle without blowing my top in front of everyone.

To cut this story short, everything went fine even though there was a procedure done without my prior knowledge or consent as part of this test, which should have been explained to me in advance. This really upset me because I felt I had been emotionally violated because surely it wouldn't have taken too long to tell me what was going to be done. I'm not the type of person that faints when told all the messy details. Luckily for me, my local doctor had been great, so I went and had a talk with him about the whole mess. He was far from happy about the way things had been handled and told me to make sure that I let the professor know what had gone on.

It seems that these people forget that they are dealing with human beings and not some emotionless puppets that have no feelings or memories. Well, I'm now at the point of only having one attempt left to have a child, with an embryo given to Ian and me by a very special couple and I'm in the process of having everything checked out to make sure that we have the best chance possible of being successful.

My heart felt as if it was in two pieces. Part of it was telling me there wouldn't be any children, despite all of the time and effort I had put into this part of my life, but at least I knew that I had put my heart and soul into it and nobody could say I didn't. I felt that I have been very persistent, regardless of all the hiccups that I had to endure along the way. I had one remaining hope and that was if things didn't work out for us to be parents, Ian and I wouldn't be judged with constant horrible remarks. People who say things have no idea of what they are doing to us emotionally. I had to be very honest in the fact that if I couldn't get this last attempt to work, I had no idea how I would handle the grieving process because of what had happened with the first three doctors, who were meant to be helping me. As far as I could see, these doctors should have realised they were in a very privileged position. After all, we didn't have to ask for their help.

If by some miracle it did work, I would never be able to repay the donor couple for what they were giving to us. I really wished that people would realise that the most important things in life cannot be bought or measured with money.

One of my favourite songs is Leningrad. It has so many different emotions in it and at the end the most dominant emotion is compassion. I just wish more of humanity was like this and the world would be a lot better for it.

Being given a child is the most precious gift a person can be given in their lifetime and if my last attempt to carry a child works, I will always have to remember that I have been entrusted to love and protect someone else's child.

2006-2008

This is the chapter of this book, that I wasn't sure would be written. I had severe doubts because I didn't know if I would have the emotional energy or desire to write it.

Ian and I now only had one opportunity left to have a child. It's very hard to put on paper, all the emotions that I was feeling at this point. To me it felt in some ways, as if I had to attend a funeral of someone very special, someone who I could not imagine living without. In this case, I knew that this phase of my life was coming to an end, and the hardest part was the fact that I had no control over the outcome.

Now there was one main issue—Ian. I had to get him to sign a consent form for the last attempt as our current form had expired. Was I in for the emotional fight of my life! I just could not figure out what Ian had to gain by being so unthoughtful, selfish and any other word you'd like to use for him trying to beak his promise. He knew all along that I—not he—had paid for three attempts on this Donor Program, and that he had no right as far as I could see, to change his mind.

It was now that I had to do a lot of scheming because I knew that forever is a very long time. I made an appointment to see our normal GP. Despite having many talks with Ian, who, by this stage, had become more like a brick, I had a very bad feeling in regards to my chances of success. After working out what my first two attempts had cost me out of the $2,000, I went and took the remaining amount out of the joint account and put it into my own account. As Ian is very in tune with money, this was the best and most effective way to try and ensure that I got his signature on the consent form. Before our appointment, I reminded him what it was for and then all I could do was hope for the best and as someone once said "expect the worst". I did tell him that he would get the money back if he signed his consent, and if not, he could kiss his money goodbye.

I had two things that I wanted to discuss at this appointment, so at least I had a backup to stall for time while Ian made up his mind. Our GP knew what was going on and clearly could see what Ian was up to. After what seemed like ages with Ian not picking up the pen, I just picked up the paper and made some comment to make him realise that time had almost run out. I couldn't believe it, he actually gained enough strength in his right arm to sign his name. When we got outside I told him we could go and swap the money back to our joint account, and he just smiled. It was then I knew that he had known all along exactly what he was doing, and as a result of this I lost a lot of respect for him. I could not longer find any excuse for delaying my last embryo transfer. I knew that I had now done everything humanly possible to help myself.

Without telling anyone, I decided to attend the clinic in June, after Ian and I had our overseas holiday. I chose not to tell anyone as I did not want people asking questions. I really felt it would be more than I could cope with. Usually when I tried to get pregnant, I felt different emotions at different stages of the process, but not this time. I felt very withdrawn and sad as this was the last time I could ever go to the clinic.

On 30 June 2006, two embryos were transferred. This appointment was very hard because over time, most of the staff had become more like friends, and now I was about to leave for the last time. I had decided that if I did not notice any changes, I wouldn't do the blood tests as I now saw them as being pointless. My brain told me that it should work, but my heart could not see how it could, or why it should work for me. So in a sense, I felt detached from reality.

Before the two weeks following the transfer were up, I began to feel totally ill and for some time I thought that nature was playing a cruel joke on me. It was the most difficult period I'd had to endure for some time and it was now that I would have to face reality and at this point that I wished to be anyone other than myself.

On 13 July the clinic phoned to tell us that I was pregnant. Leonie was over the moon and she said that "if anyone deserved to get pregnant, it's you." In some ways the phone call didn't seem real because I was so used to being disappointed and besides, Ian already knew but told me I had to call the clinic. I guess he wanted me to hear it from them as well. One would have thought that I would have been excited, but I wasn't as I had simply been through so much over such a long period of time. In some ways I felt that it would have been less stressful had the pregnancy test been negative, as I would not have had anything to lose. Now I was terrified of being late with the vital progesterone pessaries which had to be used three times a day.

During the first weeks I had to have blood tests to check how the hormones were rising. At least I could now get some understanding of why I was feeling so ill with morning sickness. At this stage, I was still doing my junk mail walk twice a week and had decided to stop in October, as the baby was due at the end of March.

On 9 August I went to the Clinic for a scan to see how many embryos had taken, as I had as chance of having twins. The Professor did the scanning and there was one little heartbeat, beating very strongly. I had mixed feelings, as March seemed so far away.

When I was getting changed after the scan I could hear the Professor ask where I was but I didn't take a lot of notice. When I went to leave the scan room I was completely surprised as the Professor had lined up quite a few nurses who were congratulating me on my success. It was now sinking in that I was really pregnant.

It had taken me twelve years and now at last I was going to be a mother. I was almost in tears as I walked past the line up, as some of the nurses had been more sincere in their work ethic than others, and I don't like people being hypocritical.

I left the Clinic with our first scan picture and a number One Baby Bounty Bag. This bag is handed out to future mothers, but I feel it's more like a double edged sword. In one way it's very good, but to those potential mothers who lose their babies this bag would be more like a knife being put through their heart. As all the blood tests were fine, Ian and I had to just mentally adjust to the idea that we were finally going to be parents. As much as I wanted to keep hopeful and positive, I was fully aware that things can go horribly wrong.

The night of 14 August, apart from feeling pregnant, I didn't notice anything wrong. Unknown to me, this was about to change and there was no way I could have been prepared for what was to occur.

When I woke up at 4am to go to the toilet, suddenly my heart sank as I knew immediately that things were not right. While I had been sleeping, the lining of my uterus had become detached and had come through my cervix. Apart from my stomach feeling very sore, I didn't have any pain, but by the time I reached the toilet my undies were full of lining and blood. At this point a lot of the mess fell onto the floor. By this time Ian had come to see what was wrong, and I told him to ring the hospital. Suddenly there was a thud in the kitchen, and despite the fact that by this time I had started to feel shaky, especially in my legs, I knew I had to get to the kitchen as Ian had fainted and was out cold.

I don't know how I managed it, but I got the phone off Ian and spoke to the nurse who said to call the ambulance. Some how I had to get to the front door and unlock it so the ambulance staff could get in. By some stroke of luck, I got from the toilet and back again without getting mess on the cream carpet. While I was waiting for help, I was searching the floor looking for the sack that the baby would have been in, but I couldn't see it.

Things had happened so quickly that I had not had the time to think that our baby was most likely dead. With Ian still on the floor, I was attended to first and when I was nearly ready to leave the house, Ian was suppose to be getting up!

This could be a story in itself, as it was very quickly decided that he would have to be picked up later, after I had been taken to the hospital. Once the hospital staff had been informed of my condition the ambulance returned to collect Ian, who, at this stage, was still on the floor!!

One of the doctors came in and checked me and decided that he could not tell if I was still pregnant. After a while I heard the ambulance return with Ian.

My happy days", Ian's voice could be heard before he got through the ambulance entrance "my head, my head" he was saying. What I never realised was that he had knocked the side of his head on the table edge as he blacked out, before landing on the floor. Picture this! The two of us lying in casualty together, waiting until the doctors came back in so then we would have some idea of what was going on.

It was now that my mind was starting to realise the predicament I found myself in. I was thinking to myself; "this is great, what am I going to tell the donating couple? Oh! Thank you very much for your donation, but sorry, I really screwed up".

As the day went on, what had happened started to sink in. Just after lunch-time, I was taken 60kms by ambulance to have a scan to check whether or not the baby had died. As part of this scan, a person is meant to drink one litre of water, one hour beforehand. Well, this was nearly more than I could cope with as with a full bladder against a very sore cervix, the pain became almost unbearable. At which point I was now broken hearted with the thought that my chance of motherhood would most likely be gone forever. I expected that the scan would just confirm my fears. How wrong could I have been?

I could not believe what I saw; our baby's little heart was still beating. On the return trip to the hospital, all I could do was look at the small scan picture.

I spent the next five days in hospital and as much as I tried to be positive, I was now too scared to move. The thought of having to go to the toilet was nearly too much as I was terrified what might be on the toilet paper. Besides all this, Ian was still recovering and could not go to work for a week or so. I could not see how I could get through the next seven months and I was now wondering whether or not Ian and I would even get to take our baby home.

It was now that I had to spend my days with my feet up to try and avoid any pressure on the cervix. My days consisted of being on our bed with everything handy so I only had to get up for toilet breaks. People were very kind and sometimes I was brought lunch. The only time I allowed myself to be out of bed for very long was to get our tea ready.

During this time, which seemed to go on forever, I soon learnt that one can only be in one position for so long, before muscles start screaming out "move me, move me!". I began to run out of options before deciding to move to the lounge room to sit in our recliner, particularly as this option came with being able to watch TV. The days went by quicker and I didn't feel so isolated. So much for being a social person, it didn't take too long for me to start missing social interaction. I was given some wool to work with, so I started to make a big baby blanket out of squares and most days I got one or more done. Most people count weeks or months in pregnancy, but I felt I could only count in days.

Everything seemed to be going well until Sunday 10 September. I had been having a morning sleep and to my horror I ended up calling the ambulance again for the same reason as the first time. As much as I thought "not again" it very quickly crossed my mind that at least Ian wasn't at home this time, which in some ways was a great relief.

As luck would have it, my regular doctor was on call and when the hospital staff phoned to call him back, he thought "Oh no—not again!" With me being, or meant to be, twelve weeks pregnant, it was hard to hear our baby's heartbeat, so the next day I went for another scan to check things out again.

Our baby had survived again, against all odds. This time, he/she was moving their arms, so back to our local hospital with another scan photo. We could not believe our luck and some of the reactions from my support network were priceless, to the point that we were almost too scared to breathe. As for the doctor, he just shook his head in amazement as by now, I had lost about a half a litre of blood over the two occasions, which does not do anything for your energy levels. We now knew what was causing the problem, and that was the fact that the placenta had attached right next to my cervix, instead of in the upper part of the uterus.

After another stay in hospital, I settled into my rather predictable routine. I felt very relieved when each week passed by without any more things going wrong.

In my mind I tried to focus on the fact that if I could stay pregnant until Christmas, the baby would have a good chance of survival. Ian and I did get to Adelaide for a couple of days, but even though I was happy to get away from home, I couldn't really relax. At this stage, the 22nd of March didn't seem that far away, so I was not so scared anymore, regardless of the fact that I had now also developed gestational diabetes! In one way this was hard for me, as I had to go 'cold turkey' on all sweet foods. If I couldn't keep my sugar levels down, I might have ended up having to go to Adelaide for our baby's arrival. This was the one thing I dreaded, because there was no way I felt that I could trust strangers with our baby.

It was at this stage that Sharon, the nurse from the Reproductive Clinic, sent us some photos of our donor's current children, so we would have some idea of what our baby was going to look like. I don't think people understand how frightening it can be when you are carrying a baby, and you have no idea of what he/she will be like. I couldn't believe that we were going to be so lucky to get such a sweet looking baby. When a person has tried so hard to have a child, you really don't care what sex it is, as long as it's alive.

One Wednesday when I was laying on our bed, someone rang and said they were horrified that I wanted our baby born at our local hospital. I personally could not see anything wrong with this plan, as I knew that I could be sent to Adelaide if I needed specialist treatment, and besides, with my past history of abuse, I felt that my local doctor had the right personality and mannerisms for me to feel comfortable with him, and for me that was very important.

The person stated, I could stick with my chosen doctor, but I would also be close to the local funeral director, I could only assume they meant for our baby. This statement was very upsetting and I couldn't believe just how horrible a person could be. Besides, how insulting was that to my doctor's intelligence and years of training? I don't like it when decent and caring people have bad stuff said about them.

At 33 weeks, I had to have yet another scan to check where the placenta was positioned, as if it was too low, I would need to go to Adelaide and I would not be able to give birth naturally.

It seemed luck was still on my side with this problem, as the placenta had moved. I was very happy as I was determined, despite my age of 45 years, to try the natural approach first, especially as I knew this would be our only child.

Things were going well up until midnight on 22nd February. I just thought I had to go to the toilet, well, I was wrong. The sack around the baby had ruptured with a flow like Niagara Falls! It just went on and on. When I did manage to get to the phone, I was advised to get to the hospital as soon as possible. We now knew that our baby's birthday would be 23rd February. Four weeks early.

I had to drive myself as Ian was harvesting grapes and wouldn't be home for some time. As soon as I opened the front door, Harry, the kitten from next door, rushed in and as I couldn't bend over, I just had to let him stay in the house until Ian got home. So much for me thinking that

Ian would realise something was on; oh dear, how wrong could I have been!

Despite the fact that I had left the house lights on and Harry inside, and the car gone from the house, Ian didn't even miss me! Forget the fact that I wasn't in our bed, Ian still didn't miss me! Help!!

When I arrived at the hospital I was met with a wheel chair and taken to room 16. After being monitored for a couple of hours, our doctor came in to check things. "It will be on today", he remarked, and then stated that he was going home for some sleep. I thought to myself "good luck".

I didn't really get back to sleep, and at 4.00am I must have had a twinge of pain, as I jumped, so that was it for any decent sleep for me. As for contractions, what contractions?

Ian and I had attended ante-natal classes, but what was happening to me didn't even come close to what I expected. My perfect birth plan went out the window.

By now the sun was coming up, and I wasn't feeling 100%. Around this time the doctor came back to see how I had advanced and if my blood pressure was rising, and whether or not the baby was in a hurry with its arrival plan. I was put on a drip with drugs to try and stop my blood pressure rising, so I wouldn't have convulsions. The side effects were dreadful I literally blew up like a puffer fish with my feet and hands being twice their normal size, and I was feeling all hot and sweaty. The thought crossed my mind, how on earth am I going to be able to push out this baby feeling like this?

By the time Ian had come in, it was early morning, and I was feeling so awful, I kept asking him why, because I still hadn't had any contractions. When the doctor came back in, he had a consent form for an emergency caesarean. I wasn't even interested in asking questions, which shows there was something very wrong with me. I simply signed the papers with what I believe to be my worst signature. I can only assume that the doctor was holding up two fingers when he asked me how many could I see and I really couldn't be bothered reading what I was consenting to.

Finally, on 23rd February 2007, at 12.08pm, our baby Derlerean was born.

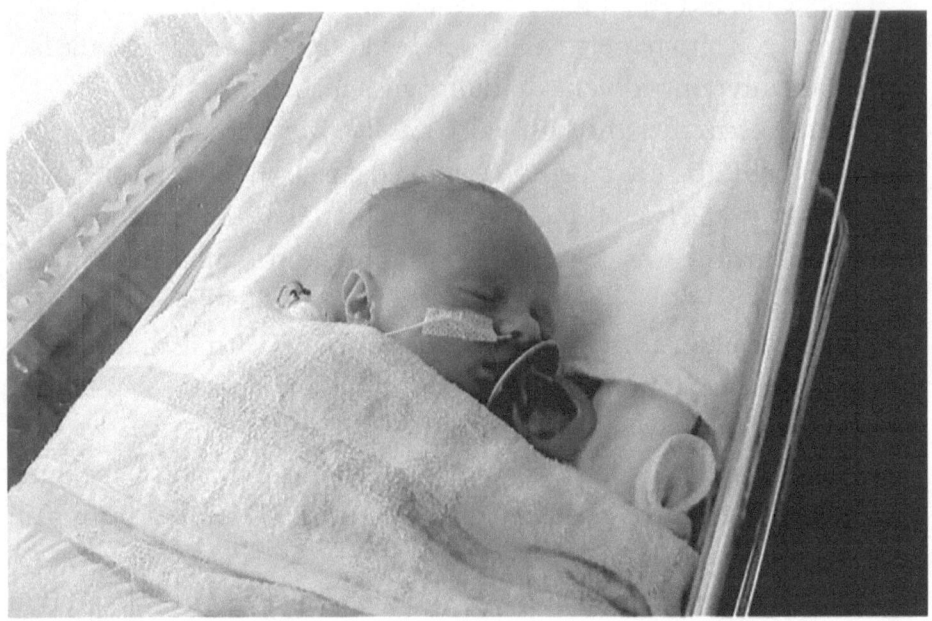

Derlerean who was only filling half of the whole baby crib. In some ways our first few days together did not seem real, because there was no emotional high for me when he was born. To me it felt like something was missing, but for Ian, happy days! He was all over Derlerean like a rash. Poor little baby.

He was four weeks early, so he couldn't feed normally, so he had to have a nasal feed tube, with my milk. The whole feeding routine took 90 minutes, every time, for the next twelve days. As for his features, he was so sweet, with dark auburn hair, of which he had quite a bit, especially at the back of his head.

I was so scared I would drop him as his legs and arms were so tiny, that even 000000's baby clothes were too big for him. We had so many gifts, it was quite overwhelming as I hadn't realised so many people cared about us. Even Ian couldn't believe it and was wondering when they would stop arriving—gifts still arrived six months after Derlerean's birth.

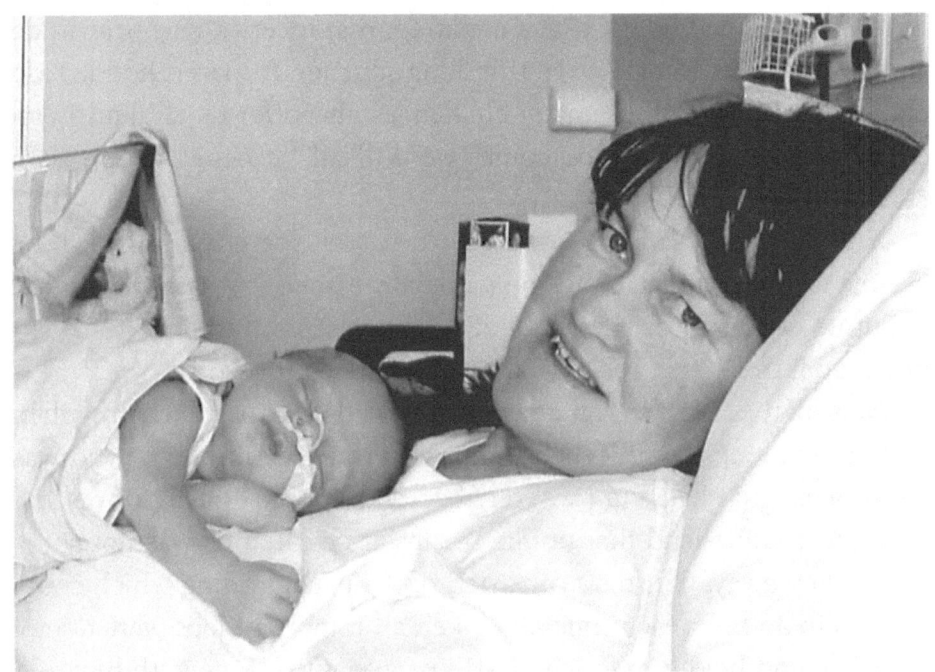

I don't know why, but I found positive comments from people hard to cope with. For example, "you're doing a great job looking after the baby", or You have a beautiful baby, or "you're lucky to have him". Despite all of these comments being true, I feel that the emotional aspects were not acknowledged. How I see it is that here I am with this precious child, that is the greatest gift of all, and yet he is not mine—mine in the sense of genetics. He will never look like me, or show any of the genetic traits I had as a child. I believe many people that have had their own families from childhood, take this for granted.

For a long time, I felt very sad inside for so many reasons, reasons which I truly believe most people would never understand, simply because they haven't had the same background as me.

I do believe that it was made worse because I felt that I had to put on a positive face so that people wouldn't think I was ungrateful, for what Ian and I had been given.

Our doctor was great, and I can honestly say that I couldn't have wished for someone better.

If I could, I would get him a medal for his sincerity, caring attitude and his support for me over this long journey to parenthood. I do realise that there will be many challenges ahead for us all, and I can only hope whatever the outcome, we will all be better people as a result.

The day Derlerean was 2 weeks old we left the hospital and did a beeline for the chemist to pick up vital baby essentials. I tried to get into a routine of sorts so Derlerean and I could sleep at the same time as I knew from the first 2 weeks what would happen if I didn't.

Most of the time I felt I managed quite well except at bath time when I felt an emotional wreck, here I am with this tiny little boy who was the greatest gift of all and I was terrified of dropping him and I was still trying to comprehend that unlike the foster children he was not going to be taken away. Our days consisted of the usual feeding which could take up to an hour each time and when all important jobs were done I would sit and hold him for ages as I knew that this time with him as a small baby was very short and was to be treasured as he would be our only child. Apart from his reflux problem, he didn't have any other issues so we were very lucky. We both enjoyed being new parents, taking him out when possible.

Ian was great at being able to get him to sleep in the evenings, but it was after this that I would wake up to any little noise consequently I had a lot of broken sleep which later lead to getting depression. This made me feel angry as I wanted to have more energy to do things with him. What made it worse was that Ian didn't understand and some comments were not very helpful. However I soldiered on as I could not give up on our little man. I had times when I felt very isolated due to being a first time older mother as I did not know anybody else in the same position. I do believe that not having any connection with my own Mother didn't help either. With no disrespect to my current foster Mum, its not the same as there has been no continuity in regards to my part in the generations—the past or future through no fault of mine.

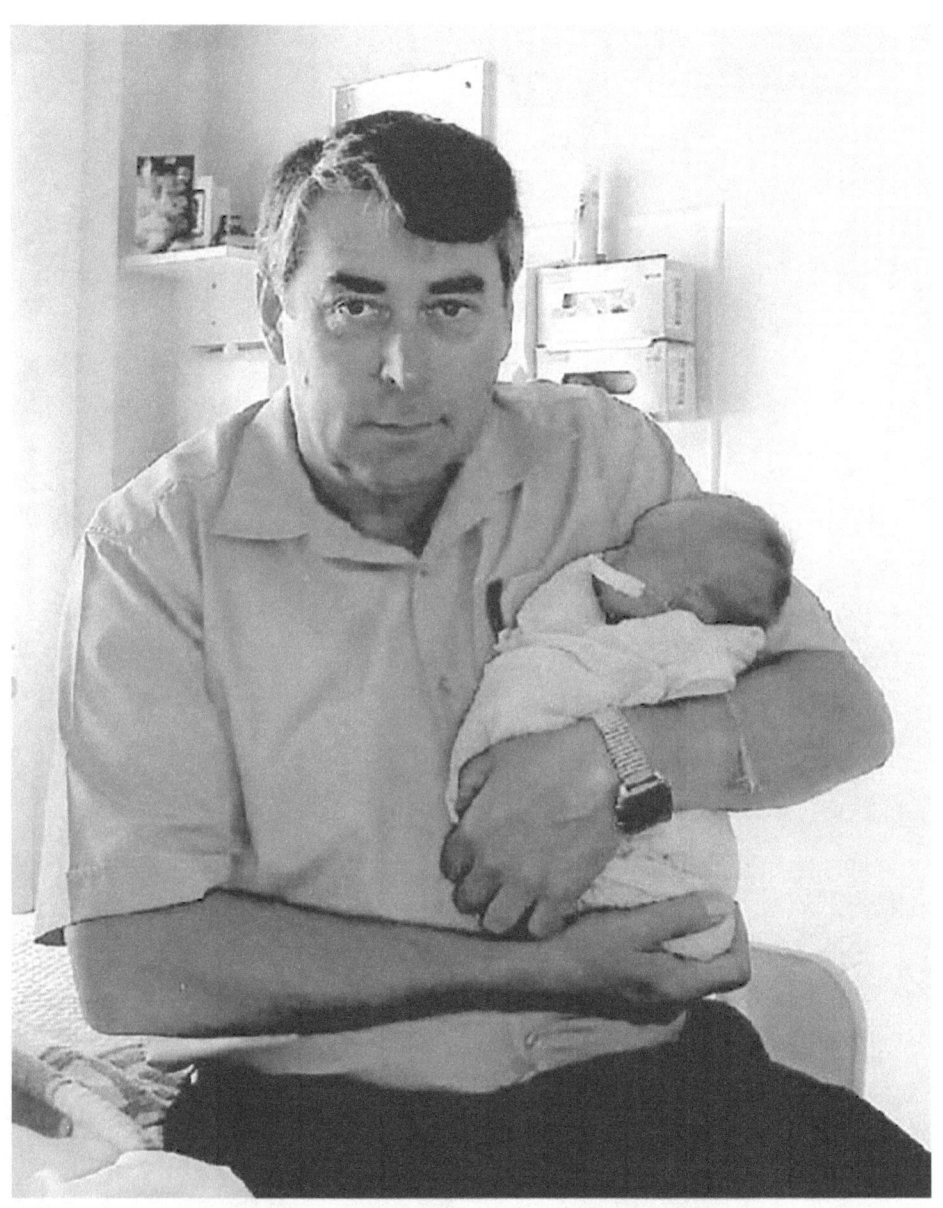

Our Family Doctor

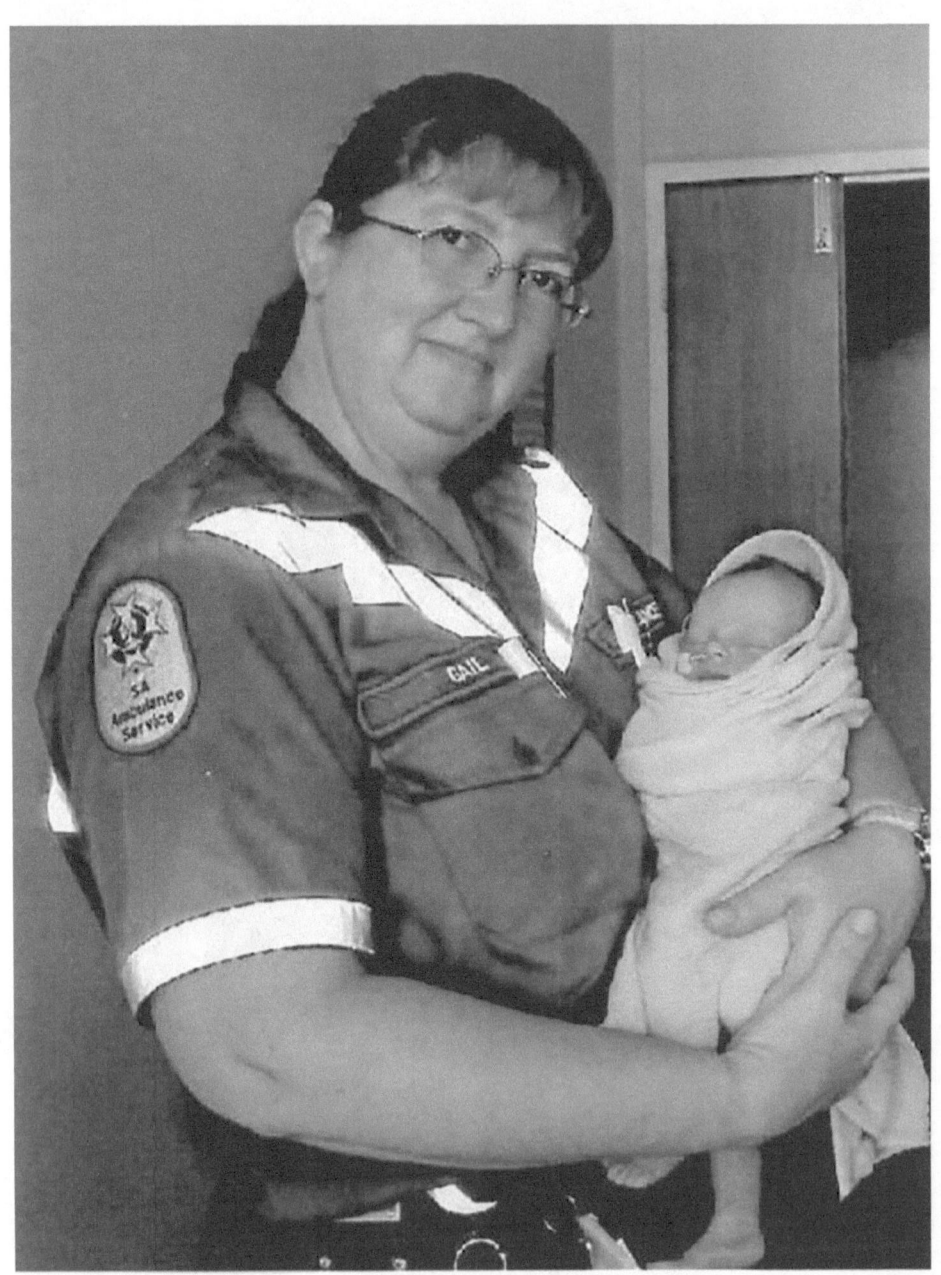

Gail and Derlerean

We enjoyed taking Derlerean shopping for clothes and the toys I felt he must have developed. At 5 months he had his first plane flight in the Air Ambulance to Adelaide as he had bronchiolitis. We were flown out at 3:00am with Derlerean looking out of the window while I was nursing him with the oxygen over his face. To any new mother this was a nightmare time. What made it even worse was that I could not give him any breast milk because of my stress levels, Ian tried to work but couldn't because of lack of concentration so he joined us later the same day.

As Derlerean became more mobile much to my horror I discovered another recurring problem and that was I could not stand him moving his legs or touching my face when he was seated on my lap. I found this very distressing emotionally because he was not doing anything wrong and yet if I had let him continue which I could not, I would have ended up screaming due to the fact of his light touch triggering off bad memories that were gained due to being abused. How unfair! Despite this we have had many priceless moments together and as his mother I have become many things: cook, photographer, teacher and playmate just to name a few.

As for Ian being a Father to our little man he is totally saturated with love for our son which has made all of the tears, fears and other rotten experiences well worth it.

Our greatest hope is that Derlerean will grow up to be a compassionate and confident person who will be able to show others less fortunate the same level of care and understanding that was given to him by all those who love him.

DERLEREAN'S ALBUM

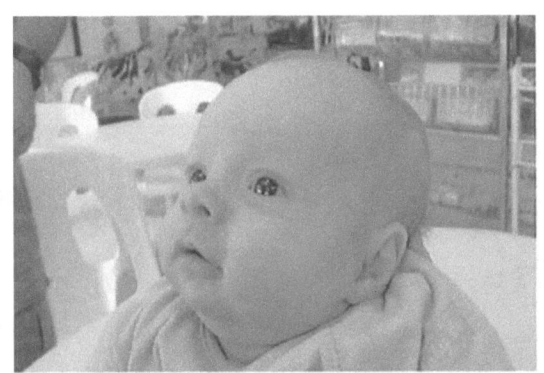

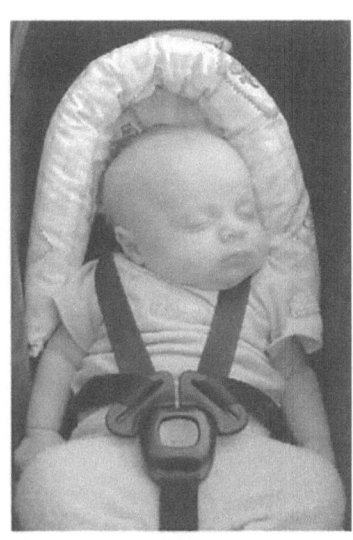

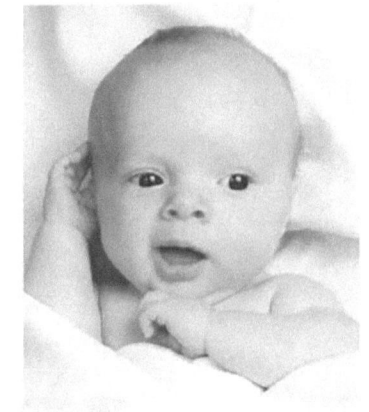

Eight week, Twelve weeks, Five months

22nd February, 2008

Our family

EPILOGUE

In 2008, I was invited to a function at Parliament House in Adelaide.

On 17th June 2008, the State Government of South Australia formally apologised to those of us who grew up in State care.

The Premier, The Hon Mike Rann MP

Requests your company

For

Morning Tea to mark the formal apology given in Parliament to people who were abused when they were children in State care.

On

Tuesday 17th June, 2008
From 10:30am to 1:00pm

At Parliament House.

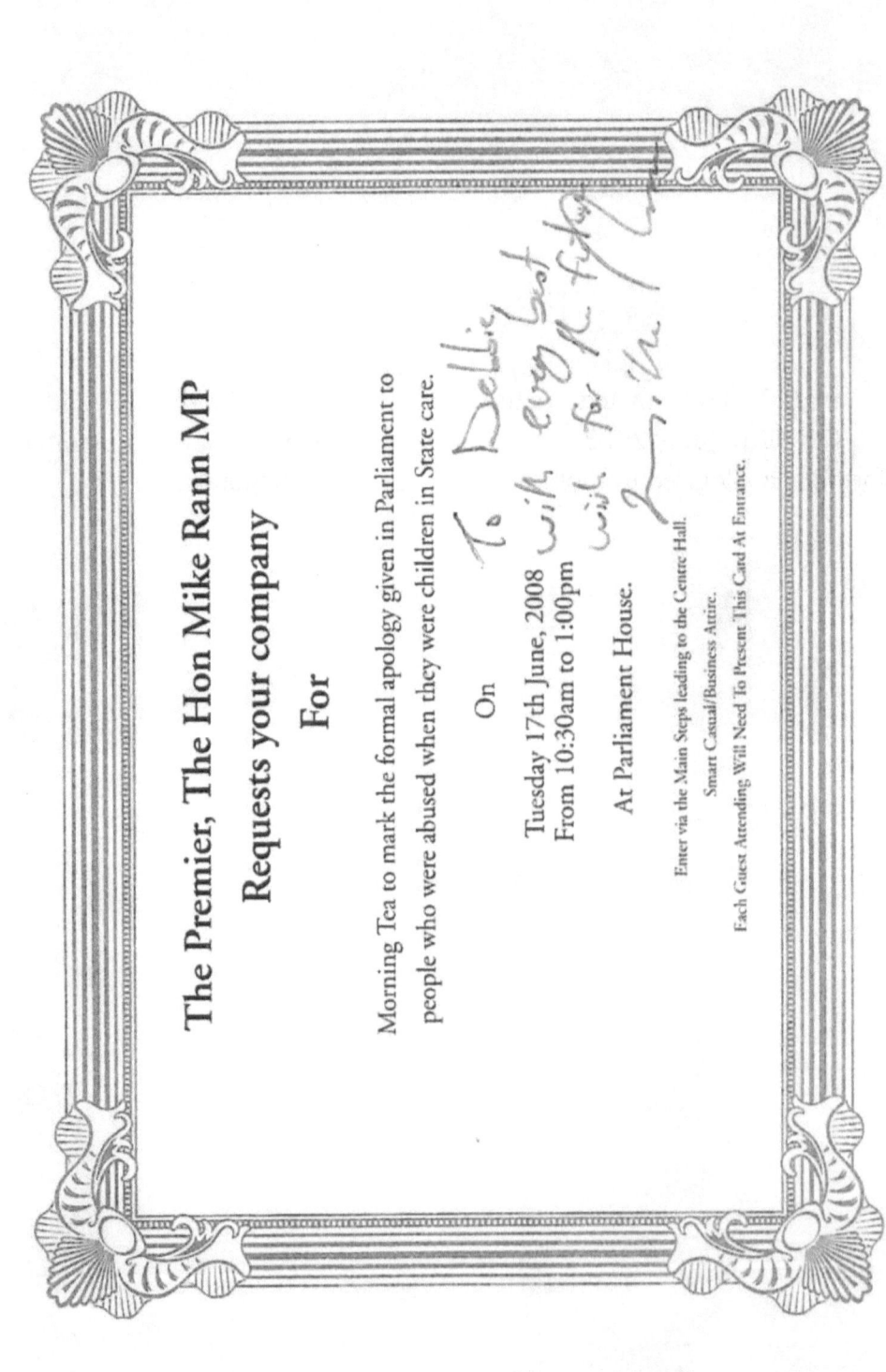

Enter via the Main Steps leading to the Centre Hall.

Smart Casual/Business Attire.

Each Guest Attending Will Need To Present This Card At Entrance.

The words of the Apology follow:

> I believe it should be accepted in the spirit in which it was
> given. The current generation of political leaders must not,
> and cannot, be held responsible for the negligence of those
> in the past.

> Debbie

Shared Government and Church apology To Those Harmed in State Care in South Australia during their Childhood

We the Government of South Australia and the Churches recognise that some children and young people who were placed in our care suffered abuse that has impacted on their lives. This should never have happened.

We are sorry and we express deep regret for the pain and hurt that they experienced through no fault of their own.

We acknowledge that in the past some carers and others who have worked in the area have abused the trust that was placed in them.

We acknowledge that the policies and practices in the last century did have a detrimental effect on some who grew up in State care.
To all those who experienced abuse in State care, we say sorry.
To those who witnessed these abuses, we say sorry.
To those who were not believed, when trying to report these abuses, we say sorry.

We are sorry for the pain shared by loved ones, husbands and wives, partners, brothers and sisters, parents, and importantly, their children.

Our apology is given in a spirit of reconciliation and healing and with our commitment to contribute toward a child safe environment in our Government, our Churches and the broader community.

We commit to do all that we reasonably can to ensure that children in our care are not subject to abuse and that those who have abused are brought to justice.

Hon Mike Rann MP
Premier of South Australia

The Most Rev'd Dr Jeffrey Driver
Archbishop of Adelaide

Rev Rod Dyson
Moderator of Synod of South Australia
Chairperson of Presbytery of South Australia
Uniting Church in Australia

Hon Jay Weatherill MP
Minister for Families and Communities

Rev Robert L Voigt
President - Lutheran Church
South Australia and Northern Territory

The Most Reverend Gregory O'Kelly SJ
Auxiliary Bishop
representing Archbishop Philip Wilson DD
Catholic Archdiocese of Adelaide

Commissioner James M. Knaggs
Territorial Commander
The Salvation Army Australia
Southern Territory

When we have passed from this life, we will be remembered - not for the things we have left behind - but for what we have given from our hearts.

— Debbie

www.ingramcontent.com/pod-product-compliance
Lightning Source LLC
Chambersburg PA
CBHW021634120626
46545CB00002B/538